. . . a nostalgia book about the football careers of Mel Triplett, Bill Triplett, and Bob Babich.
They overcame personal setbacks, illnesses, and injuries on their way to stardom.

RON "TANK" ROTUNNO

Steel Valley Books
383 Case Avenue
Sharon, PA 16146

ISBN 0-936369-51-5

"Full Tilt To The NFL"

PREFACE

This is a new experience for me, writing a preface to a book. But I'm happy to have the opportunity, because the book tells what football meant in the lives of three men who played it in high school. It also tells about the professional life of a man I consider a friend, Mel Triplett. Mel always has been a man to respect. I'm glad part of his achievements are described in this book.

Most of the players I've known wouldn't have finished high school or gone to college if they hadn't played football. I wouldn't have. I went to five different high schools when I was a kid, and football gave me a sense of security I wouldn't have had otherwise. New kids on the block usually find a change from one town to another hard. But football made the changes easy for me.

High school football teaches three things that I don't believe can be taught anywhere else: discipline, self-confidence, and self-improvement. Out on those practice fields, a youngster can actually see improvement in himself from week to week. Whether he's trying to tackle the ball carrier, catch a pass, or throw a spiral, he learns that good feeling that comes from knowing "this week I did it better." He learns he can improve the team if he improves himself, and that's something a lot of people never learn.

Also, if he has the right kind of coach, a youngster can learn discipline. That is, he can learn to follow orders or, even better, he can learn self-discipline. Frankly, I don't see that being taught much in public schools any more. I've come to think football is about the only place left where it <u>can</u> be taught. Also, I believe that teaching good sportsmanship--how to play <u>by the rules</u>--and teaching discipline has failed most in the <u>big city</u> schools. Not in the small towns. Kids in small towns learn there are rules to <u>every</u> game, not just football. And if you break the rules you get tossed out of the game. That's life. And that's football--or should be.

Football teaches self-confidence. Confidence on a team gives players confidence in other areas of their lives, too. They learn that if they can do well in one thing, they can do well in something else if they stick with it. And that's something no number of pep-talks can do. Hearing about confidence and <u>knowing</u> about confidence are two different things.

High school football can teach those three things. For a lot of young fellows, that may be all they'll ever get. Maybe all they'll ever need. But if they learn those three-- discipline, self-confidence, and how to improve--football will have made a big difference in their lives.

One other thing: for thousands of young men, football offers the chance to get a college education. And with today's dependence on technology, a college education is the most important thing available anywhere. They will be tempted to go into professional ball before graduation. But I would encourage every college athlete to <u>stay</u> in college for that degree. A professional athlete's career is short, about three and one-half years. If he doesn't have a college education, he ends up with no career and no future.

Of course, football is fun. I love it. I'd play it all over again if I could. Tom Landry said recently that one of the things about football was the chance to lose <u>without losing the will to win</u>. That's true. It's fun to win, and it's good to have friends with you when you lose. High school football also gives kids a shot at the bright lights and cheers -- and we all could use that a few times in our lives. Coaches need to drill it into their players, though, that there's more to life than football. (Some coaches need to learn that, too.) Players are often exploited by the "system," by coaches under pressure to win. Some coaches encourage kids to play when they're injured, sometimes damaged for life. And that's <u>bad</u> football.

Football kept me in high school when I would have quit. It gave me a college education and a solid, exciting career in pro ball. Whoever reads this book will learn that there's a lot of ways to go in life, and that for a few high school players, football can be one of the best.

Don Maynard
El Paso, Texas - August, 1991

CONTENTS

ACKNOWLEDGMENTS

I want to thank Larry King and his nighttime radio show for encouraging me to write this book. Also, I owe special thanks to Martha Eckman, technical-writing professor (ret.), for her professional advice.

Many people gave me valuable time and assistance: Coach Johnny Knapick and Commissioner Cecil Duffett of the Steel Valley Conference; librarians Pete Fierle and Sandy Self of the Pro Football Hall of Fame; President Bob Carroll of the Pro Football Research Association; Historian/Curator Pat Harmon of the National College Football Hall of Fame. Evelyn "Mom" Swartz gave me her understanding and moral support. And I owe a special debt of gratitude to Jimmy "Pine" Miller, who gave me access to his personal collection of sports magazines and books.

Also, to Sharon, PA, City Councilman Lou "Peach" Rotunno for his strong support of this book from its beginning.

To Florence (Ward) Biros for her God given sacrifices that helped put the book together.

To Phyllis Knapp for her patience and cooperation when she keyboarded the entire first copy of the book manuscript.

And to Donna Jackson for her cover design and typesetting of the final manuscript.

I am most grateful to the reference department staff at the Akron Public Library, Ravenna Public Library, Kent Free Library, Kent State University (PIAS), and the Youngstown Public Library. All were most helpful with suggestions and research materials.

DEDICATION

This book is for Dave "Red" Leiner
- wounded in Vietnam -

INTRODUCTION

In the fall of 1950, on a mild September Friday night, the Steel Valley Conference held its first football games. All of them started a little after sundown. About 7:30, the time local steel mills tapped furnace heats, manufacturing America's best steel.

The idea for a Steel Valley conference came from a collective group of educator's/coaches. While they were standing around talking in the boiler room of Hubbard High School in 1948: Paul Lisse (Struthers City School District), Howard W. "Howdy" Heldman (Struthers High School), Clyde "Mose" Hall (Hubbard High School), and Johnny Knapick (Campbell Memorial High School). But it takes time to get something like a sports conference organized. Lisse was the superintendent of the Struthers City School District at the time. Struthers--a suburb of Youngstown, Ohio--is in the heart of the region's steel-production valley. Lisse and his group introduced the idea to colleagues from other school districts. Sure enough, all of the head coaches and school principals--from the seven districts represented--agreed to join each other and organize the confer-ence.

A year later, newly elected officials of the conference recog-nized the following seven school districts surrounding Youngs-town as charter teams:

Austintown Fitch,   Niles McKinley,
Boardman [1951]   Campbell Memorial,
Girard, Hubbard, and Struthers.

A remarkable football tradition began with the first kickoffs that Friday night. Football seasons came and went during the next 45 years. But in those years, Steel Valley Conference football wrote some indelible parts of the region's history.

Outstanding coaches and great athletes built SVC football traditions, of course. Each had his own personal commitment to excellence and to victory. But the basis of Steel Valley traditions was always community support--on both the personal and commercial levels.

For example, WBBW Radio Station always gave good coverage to SVC's weekly games. It always broadcast scores and conference standings. Also, it presented the Ingot Award Trophy to the SVC champion each year. On a personal level, fellow students, players' families, and community sports fans always formed strong, diversified support groups each year.

In addition, star SVC football players--heroes of their day and time--conquered tough obstacles simply to play the game. To win glory and excellence for their teams. To achieve personal goals and personal visions of excellence.

They are the heart of Steel Valley tradition. This book is about three of those players: problems they faced, victories they won.

Melvin C. Triplett played in the Steel Valley Conference. He starred for Girard High School during the 1950 football season, the SVC's inaugural year. After graduation, he received many football-scholarship offers and, in 1951, chose to attend Toledo University. Mel enjoyed a great collegiate career at Toledo. From there, he went on to play outstanding seasons in the NFL with the New York Giants and Minnesota Vikings.

From 1955 to 1957, William C. Triplett, too, was a great running back at Girard High. Mel had encouraged his brother to play football during high school. Football was, for both of them, a means to a college education. After his senior year in high school, Bill, too, received college football-scholarship offers.

But Bill didn't want to attend the same university Mel had. So, to stay close to home, he chose Miami (Ohio) University. There, Triplett set collegiate records as a star halfback. After graduation, he was drafted into pro football. He played some great years for the St. Louis Cardinals, New York Giants, and Detroit Lions.

What about defensive players? The most outstanding was Bob Babich. Some folks believe Bob Babich was the greatest linebacker who ever played in the Steel Valley Conference. He went to Campbell Memorial High School and played under the tutelage of two fine coaches: Johnny Knapick and Sloko Gill.

After graduation, Babich attended Miami (Ohio) University on a football scholarship. While there, he had a fabulous career under legendary head coach Bo Schembechler. Drafted in his senior year, Babich played four years for the San Diego Chargers, then was traded to the Cleveland Browns. He was an outstanding pro middle-linebacker.

What you will find in this book is a condensed record of the professional lives of these three men: Mel Triplett. Bill Triplett, and Bob Babich. Their backgrounds. Where they came from. What setbacks and disappointments they faced when they played professional football. What their coaches and teammates said about them. What characteristics they had that made them stand out from the crowd.

And, game by game, season by season, injury after injury, how did they play the game? Did their teams win or lose? Their stories could probably come from lots of small towns in America. All schools have them: a few kids who love football, who refuse to quit when they lose. Who recognize excellence and want to achieve it for themselves. Who listen to the voices of coaches, teachers. Regardless of what their talents are, they have dreams beyond the cheers and pageantry of a football field.

These three stories just happen to be the ones I know because I learned to love the game in the Steel Valley. You will know the stories and the dreams of others--and of your own.

When Mel, Bill, and Bob played high school football, cities in the Steel Valley were booming. The sky turned bright orange-red every time steel workers tapped a furnace heat--every four to 10 hours. Everyone could hear the noise of steel banging through the mills. Inner-mill railroad cars hauling scrap metal into and new heavy steel away from the factory yards. But during the 25 to 30 years these men were playing professional football, changes came to the Steel Valley.

Mel Triplett saw it coming. He wanted to go back home and lead a program of slum clearance. Bill Triplett saw it coming. He tried to keep young people in high school, knowing education was their only hope for the future. Bob Babich saw it coming. He saw the need to work with inner-city youth groups and parole officers, trying to salvage some of the kids for the future.

The world has changed since the Tripletts and Babich played the game. If you drove through the Steel Valley today, you would see highways lined with the ruins of steel mills. Blast furnaces in shambles, torn down. Huge 15-, 50- and 300-ton cranes, electric furnaces, all the massive pieces of equipment are idle, rusting.

Factory towns have fallen victim to our changing economy. America no longer leads the world in steel production. The "rust belt" has lost population. Families have moved away. Old homes are vacant. Frequently, all that remains is a football tradition: the memory of heroes. Photographs and trophies in glass cases at the high school. Scrapbooks and high school annuals. Old newspaper clippings.

What did Mel Triplett, Bill Triplett, and Bob Babich give to the Steel Valley? What kept them going when times were tough? Where did they find the <u>will</u>, the single-minded determination to set goals and achieve them? Even when injured so badly they couldn't play, they didn't quit.

My questions in writing this book have been, game by game, and season after season:

o How did these men overcome hardships, physical injuries or illness, and play with honor and self-respect?

o What can their performances tell us? What have they given young people that they can apply in their own lives?

o Can young people or adults achieve their dreams today, like the ball players did 30 or 35 years ago?

FROM THE DELTA

Cotton, cotton, cotton.

"I worked that farm from sun up till sun down. Sometimes I fell asleep on the porch and never went to bed at all. It made a man of me. but if I never see that farm again it will be too soon."[1]

When he was playing first string fullback for the Giants--years after leaving the farm--Mel remembered those early days. He felt the years on the farm were "miserable" ones and always tried to forget them. But when he spoke about life there, he said. "It always reassured me that playing professional football is the easiest work I ever had."[2]

"When I was 6 years old," he said, "I was working a plow with two mules. When I was 9, I worked a plow and four mules just like my father. When work time came we forgot about football. Football? It was only a word to me. All I knew was cotton, cotton, cotton. I would probably still be there if it was not for those tornadoes."[3]

In 1944, a group of tornadoes hit Indianola in Sunflower County, Mississippi. Mel remembered the devastation to the cotton crops. Discouraged, Mel's dad decided to move his family to Girard, Ohio. He could find a job there in a steel mill. Things were hard that first year for Mel Triplett. To begin with, he had to adjust to city life and Ohio's compulsory school laws.

"I had been used to working so hard," he said. "that I couldn't wait to become 16 so I could quit school and go to work in the mill. The men were earning $1.25 an hour there, and on the farm we had to work a full day to earn that much. And the school in Ohio was pretty rough for me. The other kids teased me because I was two years older than my classmates. But the book work started to come easy and I didn't mind being teased."[4]

<u>Girard.</u>
Triplett also got interested in football that same year. One of 12 children, Mel tagged along with friends to football practice

one afternoon. The coach was impressed with Mel's size and asked him to try out for the team.

"I told him it looked like rasslin' to me," Triplett said.

So the coach said, "Okay, wanna rassle?"

"I told him I'd try."

The coach gave Mel a helmet and a set of shoulder pads. Put the team's two biggest linemen in front of him. Then the coach asked Mel to fight through them and tackle the ball carrier.

"I knocked one forward, the other back, and got the ball carrier," Mel said. *"Coach said, 'You sure you never played football before?' I told him I hadn't. So he asked me to try it again. This time the player I knocked back, I pulled forward, and vice versa. Then, I got the ball carrier."*[5]

Right there, the coach stopped practice and set up a race. Triplett against the team's fastest backs. Triplett won the 100-yard dash, and the next day the coach gave him a new uniform. Mel Triplett's football career had begun.

Triplett rushed for 982 yards and scored 18 touchdowns in eight games that year. He set many Girard High records in 1950, his senior football season. In the inaugural year of the Steel Valley Conference, Triplett received All-Steel Valley Conference honors as an outstanding fullback. He earned a place among the all-time great Ohio athletes and helped set "football tradition" in the Steel Valley Conference.

Actually, Mel built a more significant record <u>off</u> the field than he did <u>on</u>. Imagine this guy. He had to work 40 hours a week in a steel mill during his junior and senior years in high school. On top of that, he played football, basketball, baseball, ran track, and participated with the gymnastics team.

Coach Don Greenwood personally recruited Triplett to Toledo University after those record high school days. Trip received 26 football scholarship offers. Finally, he chose Toledo, turning down offers from much larger schools. When reporters asked why he accepted Toledo, he said, *"I thought it would be best to be a big fish in a little pond."*[6]

But Mel was also thinking about his family. His <u>own</u> family. Why? He married Gladys Bryant during his sophomore year of high school. Mel was already the father of two children before

Toledo recruited him.

University officials promised to find Mel a full-time job on top of his scholarship, so he could support his family. Mel then re-arranged his schedule. He worked from 11 p.m. to 7 a.m. at the Doehler-Jarvis Company during football season. In the off-season, he worked from 3:30 p.m. to 11:30 p.m. What a life.

"I was dead tired all the time," he said, *"but I couldn't afford to miss practice. If I had, they would have canceled my scholarship."*[7]

And his family kept on growing. By Triplett's senior year at Toledo, he was the father of three little Tripletts. Soon his wife was in the hospital after giving birth to their <u>fourth</u> child.

"When my wife was in the hospital," Triplett said, *"I took the children to football practice with me. The only one I had trouble with was Walter, who was 18 months old. I would bring along a blanket and put him to sleep behind the goal post. My other children watched him while I practiced.*

One day my little girl ran out on the field and hollered. 'Daddy, we need you!'"[8]

Apparently Walter was having a problem. Triplett raced off the field, over to a small bag lying on the ground. He groped inside for one piece of cloth. Laboriously, he changed Walter's diaper.

Obviously, as a parent, a college student, and a ball-player, Mel Triplett was determined to succeed. Other people could see that he had the <u>desire</u> to succeed and the ability to deal with adverse circumstances. Unusual ones, too. How many college students has anybody heard of who could combine baby-sitting with football practice--and a full-time job?

After outstanding games against Bowling Green and Western Michigan, Triplett led the Mid-American Conference as the top ground gainer. Opponents had to hit the big Rocket fullback nearly every play. They never knew what he might be doing. Carrying the ball or faking a hand-off through the line.

Triplett also played nose-man on defense. As a member of the Rocket one-platoon system, he did a good job of stopping inside ground plays.

<u>Hard times.</u>

Then came bad news. After 28 months at the Doehler-Jarvis Company, Triplett was laid off. What to do? What to do was: Mel looked for another job. Fairly soon, he found a new job, a 40-hour week with Continental Baking Company. Bad news, again. After several weeks, he was laid off. Same song, second verse: Mel was out looking for another place to work. That's how it went.

Amazingly, Mel was still able to stay on top of his school work while handling the rigors of football, working 40-hour weeks, and raising a family. Mel said it took about a year, at first, just to learn how to study. He failed a couple of courses in the process of learning. But eventually, he raised his grades to a C+ average. His professors commented on Mel's good memory.

"He doesn't recite much or volunteer much in class."[9] one professor reported, *"but he pays attention and never cuts. I never had any hint of how much Mr. Triplett was getting from my course until I threw a surprise examination at him. He did very well on it, and it was then I discovered that he's a far better student than I'd expected."*

Triplett captained the Toledo Rockets as a senior in 1954. That year, he rushed for 795 yards on 149 tries with a 5.3 average. He received first team All-MAC honors--was selected as the outstanding back in Ohio--and played outstanding ball in the College All-Star Game. The New York Giants drafted him in the 5th round.

<u>On to the N.F.L.</u>

When Triplett was playing for the New York Giants early in the 1956 campaign, the question arose about his running power. "Just how much power does the former Toledo University fullback have?"[10] they asked. Some football critics said Trip was just as powerful as Bronko Nagurski. Other conservative experts claimed he was the greatest since Marion Motley -- both Nagurski and Motley were Football Hall of Fame inductees.

"That's hard to rate." said Giants coach Jim Lee Howell." *He's just about as powerful as any other runner I've seen the last two years, so why not let it go at that?"*[11]

Howell spoke from his own experience as a player in the National Football League. He laughed about the criticism New

York got when they drafted Triplett in 1955.

"A lot of people said, 'There they go--picking some un-heard-of guy'," Howell said. *"Of course, a lot of full-backs more famous than Triplett were still available to us in the draft. But this fellow really was well known in pro circles and somebody else would have drafted him. We had seen films of every game he played for Toledo in 1954. So we knew what we were getting."*[12]

But the big fullback ran the ball only 34 times for 138 yards during his rookie season.

"He didn't report to us until late in training. And we had an entirely different set of signs and systems than what he was accustomed to," said Howell. *"That hurt him just as it hurts a lot of other kids trying to break into this league."*[13]

Even Triplett's teammates could not believe his terrific power as a runner. Mel would sometimes run over his own   T-Formation quarterback when taking a hand-off.

"That was very disconcerting," Howell conceded. *"I kept telling fellows around the league how this guy can run right over people, but they laughed at me. They told me I was exaggerating his power.*[14]

"Well, now everybody can see this is a guy who just takes off and keeps on going. It requires terrific power to run over a 260-pound tackle, but this guy can do it."[15]

Coach Howell laughed once more. *"He tells me he's got a little brother in Girard High School who makes him look like a broken-field runner,"* he said. *"I hope I'm around long enough to see that."*[16]

Howell didn't have any questions about Trip's power as the Giants #1 fullback. Especially after the "Human Bomb" exploded in the Giants' triumph over the Cleveland Browns. Howell tabbed Triplett as "one of pro football's future greats" following the game.

"He's got it all," Howell enthused. At 6'1" and weighing 215 pounds, Triplett scored six touchdowns in the Giants' first two games of the 1956 season. He rushed for 91 yards in 19 carries during that 21-9 victory over the Browns.[17]

"He's got the speed, the determination and--you can say

this for sure--the power."[18]

Giants coaches and teammates ranked the star fullback as a great <u>team</u> player, too. They meant that he gave a 100% effort in carrying out his assignments. And the Giants gave him a <u>lot</u> of assignments: running the ball, blocking, receiving, and taking fakes.

Thus, the 1956 New York Giants were on their way to a championship year. And Mel Triplett was an integral part of the Giants' winning tradition.

Triplett showed his importance to the Giants' team early in the season. During an exhibition game with the Los Angeles Rams, the Rams scored first. But the Giants tied the score later in the first period. Completing a 15-yard drive, Triplett blasted through L.A.'s defense from the 1-yard line. And the Giants went on to win that game, 20-10.

<u>Opening season</u>.

<u>San Francisco</u>. The Giants opened the regular season on the road with a 38-21 victory over the San Francisco 49ers. The Giants scored the first three times they had the ball. Amazing. The first score came from a 44-yard pass-run play from Heinrich to Alex Webster coming out of the backfield. Next, Frank Gifford raced down field for a 59-yard touchdown, cutting behind Giants blockers. Then Gifford scored again: a 17-yard field goal.

But the game was an even battle from that point on. Halfback Hugh McElhenny of San Francisco played outstanding football that day.

It was also a big day for #33, Mel Triplett! The powerful fullback rushed for three touchdowns, giving his team the winning edge.

In that game, Triplett attained his dream of playing pro football. It was a goal he'd aspired to in college. But being a hero in pro football was not his only ambition. His other goal was to go back to his hometown of Girard. So he could someday lead a drive for slum renovation. Because he held a B.S. degree with a major in sociology and minor in psychology, Trip seemed to be well suited for such a task.

"I want to live in Toledo, but there's that one job I'd like to get done back home,"[19] Mel said. He had his own large family at the time in Toledo. He felt partial about "home," though. Back

home, he had eleven siblings as well as his parents. But that dream was for later. In 1956, football came first.

Off and running.

Cardinals. In game #2, the Chicago Cardinals remained undefeated in the N.F.L.'s Eastern Division by beating the New York Giants. Quarterback Lamar McHan led the way for the Cards, scoring two touchdowns and passing for two others.

Did we say Chicago Cardinals? Yes. In those years Chicago had two football teams. Chicago's teams were the Bears and the Cardinals. And at the beginning of 1960, New York had two football teams. New York's teams were the Titans and the Giants. The Cardinals didn't move to St. Louis until 1960. And they now have moved to Phoenix, Arizona. O.K., with history out of the way, back to 1956.

Although the Giants started too late, Mel Triplett paced the team with another three touchdowns in one game.

Late in the fourth quarter, Triplett went over for his third score of the game. This one capped a Chuck Conerly led drive. Conerly also hit Ken MacAfee with a little 5-yard touchdown pass in the last few seconds of the game. But all the Giants' effort was not enough. The high-intensity Cardinals beat the Giants, 35-27.

Browns. The following week, the Giants traveled to Cleveland. They played the champion Cleveland Browns before 50,042 howling fans at Municipal Stadium. The fans weren't howling too much at the end, though. Alex Webster scored three times, and New York defeated Cleveland 21-9. It was their first win over the Browns in three years. More than that, Jim Lee Howell's New Yorkers didn't put on a one-man show for the Browns that day. All 31 players made an all-out effort.

> *"This was truly a team effort. up front as well*
> *as in the backfield. The blocking was excellent.*
> *the tackling crisp. and the generalship of Don*
> *Heinrich and Chuck Conerly effective."*[20]

The Giants played superior football that day and gained a lot of recognition: C.B.S. began televising selected N.F.L. games during the year across the nation. The Browns vs. Giants game was one of the first televised.

Cleveland's passing offense was their biggest threat against

New York. With a 14-point advantage late in the fourth period, the Giants had to use the clock in their favor. They played it cozy by giving the Browns a series of short passes to kill time. And the Cleveland quarterback had time to complete quite a few.

Ratterman marched the Browns to the Giants 1-yard line. And that line was where the Giants won the war. On fourth and goal, the Browns' Ed "Big Mo" Modzelewski tried to invade Dick "Little Mo" Modzelewski's turf. But Little Mo, the brother playing for the Giants, stood his ground. Little Mo prevailed, and New York made a remarkable goal line stand.

Throughout the game, Cleveland was unable to stop New York's rushing trio. With sound line-blocking, Giants backs gained consistent and crucial yardage. All three--Alex Webster, Mel Triplett, and Frank Gifford--had a great day. Triplett, Gifford, and Webster hammered their way through the Brown's defensive line.

Ratterman lifted the Browns' hope when he completed passes to Darrell (Pete) Brewster and Dante Lavelli. Lavelli was the first great end to play pro football. His nickname was "Glue Fingers" because he always caught the football.

"He never dropped a pass in practice or in a game during the eleven years I coached him", said Head Coach Paul Brown.

Suddenly, the Browns had a first down on the Giants' 14. But on two successive defensive plays, Walt Yawarsky and Andy Robustelli sacked Ratterman for big losses. Ratterman dropped back to pass. Like a shot, Yawarsky broke through to throw him for a 10-yard loss. The game was history on the next pass attempt: Robustelli hit Ratterman for a 17-yard loss.

After the Giants beat the Browns, Roosevelt Grier was in "gigantic" joke-telling form. He was, both literally and figuratively, a mountain of a man at 6'5, weighing 275 pounds. A terror on the field, Grier was usually a genial member of the Giants squad--especially after winning. Give him his football, his guitar, and his sense of humor--and Grier would tell jokes before or after a football game. But not <u>during</u>.

On down the line.

<u>Eagles</u>. Many loyal fans came to watch the Giants play the Philadelphia Eagles in Yankee Stadium. That year, the Giants

had moved from the Polo Grounds to Yankee Stadium. More fans could see more of the game. Fortunately New York's offense was good enough in key situations to beat the Eagles--and please the fans!

The Eagles scored first on Bobby Walston's 15-yard field goal. But they didn't have a backfield as good as Conerly, Gifford, Webster, and Triplett. For a while, Philadelphia's 6-1-2 defense contained New York's ground attack.

The Giants collected some injuries, however, in that hard-hitting contest. Sam Huff suffered a mild concussion when he made a tackle. Triplett sprained his left wrist while making a block. And Yawarsky injured his right knee ligaments.

Coach Howell was really happy with the team's defensive performance but felt disappointed with their offense. "We were ragged, we fumbled, and did not pass as often as we should have," he said. "Owen's defense checked our running. We should have done more passing."[21]

The Giants head coach did say, also, that the offensive executed the pitch-out maneuver play very well." ...our key play of the game"[23] Vince Lombardi, the Giants' backfield and offensive coach, drew a sketch of the play that diagrammed each man's assignment. Coach Howell explained the play:

Play:

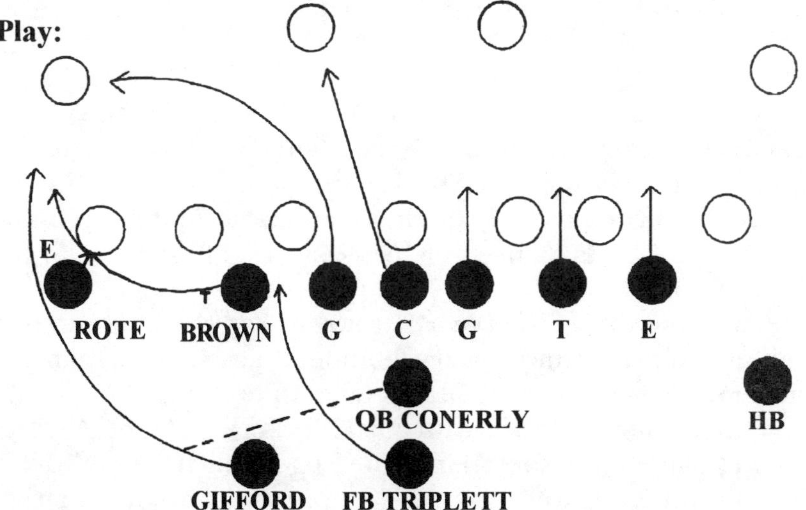

Figure 1 <u>New York Times</u>

We had been running <u>through</u> the Eagles' line mostly. This was an attempt to bring defenders closer to the middle. Make them wary of moves through guard, tackle and center. Then we figured we would have them set up for the wide sweep."[23]

In the plays before the pitch-out, the Giants ran over right tackle for yardage. Quarterback Conerly of the Giants then called the pitch-out maneuver. The Giants backfield set up in their usual T-formation, with end Kyle Rote playing wide to the left.

"Rote was not too wide, however." Howell noted. *"He had to be able to block on this play instead of running out as a decoy or pass receiver."*[24]

Another important phase of the play was Conerly's fake to fullback Triplett. Triplett hit inside tackle and guard, pulling the Eagles' defensive men inside <u>before</u> Conerly pitched to Gifford on the sweep. The Eagles were set for another Giants attack through the middle. They were just not ready for the Gifford run-sweep! Conerly made a nice fake to Triplett into the line, pulling defenders inward. Then Gifford took Conerly's quick pitch and went around left end. It was wide open for a 37-yard gain. The charging Eagles' defense had been fooled and foiled. They had no chance to stop the elusive Gifford.

<u>Down to the wire</u>.

<u>Cardinals again</u>. Toward the end of the season, the Cardinals were tied for first place with the Giants in a battle for the top spot. Fortunately the New Yorkers--6-1 after winning over the Cardinals--turned them back in their second match-up of the season, the Giants gained sole possession of first place in the Eastern Conference.

After the game, the record crowd at Yankee Stadium had nothing but praise for Howell's fabulous Giants. More than one fan said, "This is the best Giants team in ten years."[25]

The offense sparkled with good blockers up front. A super passing game gave the Giants the edge. Bill Austin's, Jerry Huth's, and Kyle Rote's blocking supported Chuck Conerly's passing. Great blocking made room for Gifford's, Webster's, and

Triplett's running, too. From the time Andy Robustelli blocked a Cards' punt by Dave Mann, early in the game, the home team was inspired to victory.

Triplett excelled both as a runner and a blocker while helping the Giants take first place in the Conference. He was a hard-driving fullback, and the Giants used him extensively. He was their "mine-sweeper," clearing the way for Webster, Gifford, and other Giant backfield men.

"Frankly," said Triplett, *"I'd rather run than block. Blocking in this league is no picnic. Most of the time I have to knock down ends and linebackers who outweigh me by as much as forty pounds."*[26]

"But every time I'm reminded of those years on that farm, I know how lucky I am now....thank the Lord for making me a professional football player."[27]

The Giants finished their campaign at the top of the Eastern Conference, (8-3-1). They won two of their last five games and played the Chicago Bears (Western Conference champions) to a 17-17 tie. The two football powers then got ready to play each other one more time for the world championship. Giants and Bears would play the game on December 30, 1956. The last time the Giants had won the championship was in 1938.

That December day in 1956, 56,836 loyal fans were shivering at Yankee Stadium in their blue, red, and white scarves, sweaters, and overcoats. They could scarcely believe New York's dominance of the Western Conference Champions. The Giants themselves found it hard to believe, too. More than that, the Giants found it hard to believe they were facing the same Bears who'd played them to a tie during the regular season.

By intermission the Giants had a 34-7 lead, and a lot of Bears fans left the Stadium, discouraged. Chicago's only touchdown came after a fumbled punt recovery on New York's 25-yard line.

The game was almost a replica of the 1934 championship game between the same two clubs. The gridiron was frozen solid in 1934, as it was for this one. But on game day in 1934, the Giants were losing until the third quarter. At that point, they changed from football cleats to basketball sneakers. With better traction, they overcame a 13-3 handicap and routed the Bears 30-13. That game is still called the "Sneakers Game." George Halas's Chicago Bears also changed to sneakers that day, but they made the change too late. The 1934 Giants won the top prize. Their first National Football League championship title!

<u>But back to 1956</u>. That December, Chicago put some all-time star players on the field: Rick Casares, Ed Brown, George Blanda, J. C. Caroline, and Harlon Hill. But they never got the Bears moving. After the Bears' only score, the New York defense contained the Bears offense for the rest of the game. On the other hand, the New York Giants had some star players, too: Charley Conerly, Mel Triplett, Frank Gifford, Alex Webster, and Kyle Rote were on offense. On defense, the Giants had Roosevelt Grier, Andy Robustelli, Dick Modzelewski, Bill Svoboda, Ray Beck, Em Tunnell, and Jim Patton.

A lot of football glory carved its way into Giants tradition on that historic victory day. Alex Webster scored two touchdowns. Triplett, Rote, Moore, and Gifford scored one each. Playing in the fourth period, Conerly threw passing scores to Rote and Gifford.

<u>Game Day</u>.

New York won the coin toss and elected to receive. On the first play of the game, George Blanda kicked a high end-over-end opening kickoff to return specialist Gene Filipski. Filipski caught it at the Giants 8-yard line. He ran the ball behind five cross-blocks for a 53-yard return to the Bear's 39-yard line. What a way to begin...

New York's first two scrimmage plays netted only one yard. A third-down pass play, however, from Heinrich to Gifford, gained 21 yards. And on the fourth play, Heinrich handed off to Mel Triplett for the Giants' famous draw play. Unleashing all his power, Triplett blasted 17 yards for the Giants' first touchdown. On his way to the end zone, Trip trampled a Chicago defensive tackle. He ran over defensive backs McNeil Moore and Stan Wallace. And he flattened umpire Sam Wilson at the goal line.

One New York sports writer described Mel's historic run: "When Mel Triplett burst through the middle for 17 yards and the Giant touchdown, he moved like a speed boat spraying water behind him. The big fellow not only sprayed Bear tacklers, but also Sam Wilson, the umpire, riding the official into the end zone with him."[28]

Triplett's smashing run into the end zone gave the Giants their initial momentum. They went on to crush the Bears 47-7.

Mel Triplett finished the day with 71 yards rushing and his first-period touchdown. Also, Trip threw some great blocks for his teammates. All in all, Triplett had a fine year.

The Giants ticket office had a big day, too. Only 6,000 tickets were sold at the gate in such bitterly cold weather. But gross receipts of $517,385, including $205,000 for television and radio rights, set a new record. Pay-offs to players in this game reached an all time high. Each winning Giant received $3,779.19. Each losing Bear player received $2,485.16, and the second place teams in the league shared $28,483.81.

Truly an emotional event. Coaches had made comments, of course, before and after the game. Coach Howell talked about his players laughing and joking before game time. Something he called "too much levity."[29]

Howell was worried about his team's morale. A soft-spoken man, he said, *"I always thought players should be pretty quiet and alone before the big game. At least that's the way we always were when I played."*

But about 4:45 p.m. that afternoon, the Giants were laughing, joking, "whooping it up." After such a great team victory, they were installing themselves as heroes.

Vince Lombardi, the Giants offensive coach said, *"We were on our way when Gene Filipski returned the opening kickoff 53 yards. That good criss-cross blocking for the runner, who went straight up the field, showed the team was out for a 33-man effort."*[30]

In the locker room after the game, Howell agreed with Lombardi's concept. *"This is the best team I've coached here since the 1948 squad and it's head and shoulders above the 1946 squad."* Nobody had to be reminded that the 1946 Giants team lost to the Bears in the world title game.

Head coach Paddy Driscoll of the Bears said it another way: *"When you run up against some fellows playing like that, there's just about nothing you can do.*"[32]

Triplett's improvement as a fullback helped the Giants a lot that year, and Coach Howell acknowledged Trip's accomplishments. At a later date, he reflected on how Mel had performed in his rookie year. *"Triplett was something of a problem as a rookie. A smashing runner and a vicious blocker, he was 6'1", weighed 215 pounds. He was the big back the Giants had always wanted. But he wasn't a good pass receiver,"* said Howell. *"He may even have fumbled on complicated exchanges ...Still, Triplett was a brute. He was a lot of man. He was also a temperamental man, whose emotions robbed him of consistency and All-Pro recognition."*[33]

BUILDING A CAREER

The best the Giants could do during the 1957 campaign was to finish second. The Cleveland Browns took top honors in the Eastern Conference that year. The New Yorkers' lack-luster defense was almost the opposite of its 1956 defense. In '56, the Giants had the best defense in the NFL against the run. They allowed their opponents just a bit more than a hundred yards per game -- about 3.5 yards per carry.

<u>Slow start.</u>

In 1957, the yardage soared. Sure, the Giants had a reason: Rosy Grier was absent from the defense. Grier had joined the U. S. Army and was stationed at Fort Dix. With Grier gone from defensive right tackle, the Giants gave their opposing teams almost 150 yards per game. On the average, 4 yards per try on the rush. At 6'5", weighing 275 lbs., Grier had been their mainstay, and they missed him sorely.

The Giants lost their first game to Cleveland at Cleveland's Municipal Stadium. In the final seconds, Lou Groza booted a 47-yard field goal that gave the Browns a 6-3 victory. Jimmy Brown made his debut as a professional player that day. He gained 89 yards rushing. The Giant's defensive men--especially the linebackers--suddenly realized: <u>here</u> was a great football player! In their next two out-of-town games, New York came through with identical victories. They defeated Philadelphia and Washington: both, 24-20.

Fans grew excited that year about changes in professional football. Rules were changing. The game was moving more toward what we know as "pro" ball today. Action from the "red dog" -- rushing linebackers through the line on defensive plays -- caught the fans' interest. Now we call it a "blitz." Then, it was a brand new concept for stopping the opponents' offense.

The quarterback "audible" was another new idea. It gave signal-callers a chance to change plays at the line of scrimmage. A judgment call against a particular defensive line-up could give the quarterback a quick advantage--like where to run or pass the football. Also, the media broadened its coverage of pro football. They gave spectators front-page sports news about all the changes taking place. And CBS's expanded-telecasts brought pro football into people's homes. Much larger numbers of fans began watching the games.

Toward the end of the season, the Browns (8-1-1) held first place in the Eastern Conference. New York still had a shot at first place, but only on two conditions. First, they would have to beat the Steelers away from home. Second, the Detroit Lions would have to defeat Cleveland in the same week. The Lions did beat the Browns in a crushing victory. But the Giants lost their match against Pittsburgh, 21-10. Gloom. That missed set of conditions wiped out the Giants' title hopes completely.

Still, while the teams were getting ready for their final game, both Giants and Browns fans reached a frenzy of excitement. Spectators from both teams saw the event as the most important of the 1957 campaign. Fan agitation and media hype grew to outrageous levels. Something like today's Super Bowl "hysteria."

One tale of the day exaggerated the rivalry between two normally competitive football teams. From the early 1950's, so the story went, the Browns and Giants always battled brutally for victory. According to the hype, one or the other could win <u>only</u> by the <u>closest</u> margin. Superstition featured heavily in the hype.

<u>Browns</u>. From the outset both teams rallied their troops to score a lot of points from touchdowns to field goals. Giant fans were curious about how their club would defense Jimmy Brown. The Browns had acquired Brown from Syracuse University in the '57 Pro Football Draft. He was their outstanding rookie fullback, and he blended speed with power.

Jim Brown's counterpart, Mel Triplett, was having a sluggish year--at least compared to his record the year before. In 1957, Triplett had only 61 carries during the whole year. In years to come, Triplett would outshine Brown in rushing yardage several times. But not in 1957.

To stop Jim Brown, New York's defensive coach, Tom Landry, assigned middle linebacker Sam Huff to key on Brown. Huff was supposed to pursue Brown every time he carried the ball -- either tackling or slowing him. Huff did tackle Brown several times, but usually Brown was hard to stop. Huff described what he had to do: *"Grab Brown, hold him, and wait for help."*

New York viewers looked on eagerly, but they were frustrated. The Giants blew a final quarter lead (28-27). As the fans watched, alarmed, the Browns suddenly went ahead, 34-28. Time was running out. The New Yorkers still had a last chance to score. Halfbacks Gifford and Webster gained impressive yardage, and New York fans were chanting, "Go! Go! Go!" But the Giants stalled on the Browns 24-yard line. Too little, too late.

Two weeks later, Cleveland lost to the Detroit Lions in the world championship game, 59-14.

<u>Hope springs....</u>
Coach Howell, thus, held little hope for his 1958 team. Especially after the Giants dropped five straight exhibition games before the regular season opened. But in game #1, the Giants pulled it together in a 37-7 win over the Chicago Cardinals. It seemed as if, once again, maybe the Giants were going to be a team to be reckoned with in the Eastern Conference. By the time game three rolled by, the Giants had a 2-1 record. They won 21-14 over the Washington Redskins at Griffith Stadium. Surely they would prove to be contenders for the Conference championship.

<u>Redskins</u>. Early in the fourth quarter, Charley Conerly threw a 10-yard wobbly--but game clincher!--pass to Ken MacAfee. Both the fans <u>and</u> the Giants were glad to take the impressive-looking score.

The Giants' defense made two fourth-quarter stands, stopping Washington once on the 2- and once on the 17-yard line. Outstanding defensive plays by Sam Huff and Cliff Livingston stopped the Redskins advance. And, during the game, New York's defense held together a pair of first-quarter touchdowns.

The explosive New York defense inspired their offense. First, Gifford swept right end for a 6-yard touchdown, following fine blocking by Bob Mischak, Frank Youso, and Alex Webster. Next, Triplett's running set up another touchdown play. The score came on Heinrich's 41-yard pass to Bob Schnelker. If the Redskins plugged-up the middle of the line, big #33 hammered out yardage time after time on the "fullback draw." That was the play Trip made famous. He fooled the Redskins: he ran it wide and quick instead of going up the middle. Washington's 14 points that day came from Jim Podoley's pass receiving, LeBaron's passing, and from Don Bosseler's and Ed Sutton's effective running.

Bragging rights?
New York fans started buzzing about maybe having world championship bragging rights that year -- in football and base-ball. In 1958, the New York Yankees were behind the Milwaukee Braves three games to one in the World Series. But the Yankees came back, surprising everybody, and won the world champion-ship. Two winning teams in New York? It was possible.

The fourth week, however, the Cardinals flew into Yankee Stadium and upset New York 23-6. It was the Giants' home opener, and it disillusioned New York spectators in a hurry.

Pittsburgh. Back at Yankee Stadium the next week, Triplett and Webster were the top ground gainers against the Steelers. In that game, the Giants triumphed over Pittsburgh 17-6. Hopes climbed back up again. Bobby Layne was playing for the Steelers then. In the rain and mud, New York's hard hitting defense made mud pies of Layne's offense. They stopped Layne every time it counted. Although Layne's passing game was good, Pittsburgh's best running back, Tom "The Bomb" Tracy, fumbled three times. And the Giants, playing heads up ball, recovered all three.

Tom Landry along with Cliff Livingston and Andy Robus-telli took credit for the victory. Also, they claimed the Giants' undisputed possession of second place in the Eastern Confer-ence. Of course, people would always remember coach Vince Lombardi's offense as a great one. Not just in the Steelers game, but in most others as well.

Still, the 1958 season was a landmark: it was the last time Tom Landry and Vince Lombardi would coach together for Jim Lee Howell. Lombardi went to Green Bay as head coach the next year. The year after Lombardi left, Tom Landry took the head coaching position with the Dallas Cowboys.

<u>Browns</u>. Next, the Giants faced an all-important game against first-place Cleveland. A record crowd came to Cleveland Stadium to watch Jimmy Brown matched against Mel Triplett. Since the first week of training camp, the Giants had been a little disappointed by Triplett's overall performance. Coach Howell even threatened to release him if he didn't begin to give a 100% effort every game.

"Mel always plays better when the other team has a superior fullback. Not necessarily superior to Mel, but out-standing," said Howell before the Cleveland game. *"The Browns have a great fullback in Jimmy Brown. With that in mind, we've been working on Triplett all week."*[1]

One of the chief "workers" was Tom Landry. Tom was a defensive genius with an acerbic wit. *"How is it Jimmy Brown gains more in one game than you gain in a whole season?"*Landry asked Triplett. *"It just doesn't make sense to me."*[2]

All the "working on" worked. Triplett was a key figure in winning the Cleveland game. By game time, he was ready to play with a 100% desire. [From Vince Lombardi, they say, Triplett gained the will to win and, with Lombardi's help, made his own personal commitment to excellence and to victory.]

Jim Brown entered the game with 15 touchdowns (NFL single-season record: 18 by Steve Van Buren). And he had 928 rushing yards (NFL record: 1,146 by Van Buren) to his credit. But with middle linebacker Sam Huff keying on Brown, the New York defense felt totally ready to stop him. The star full-back of the game, Mel Triplett, rushed for 116 yards. Jim Brown, only 113. Triplett and the whole defense received commendations for playing superbly in the Giants' 21-17 triumph.

In the Western Conference, the Baltimore Colts were also playing great football. Weeb Ewbank's Colts had trampled Green Bay 56-0. The Colts remained undefeated with a 6-0 mark. They were New York's next opponent.

<u>Baltimore</u>. At Yankee Stadium, the game had already drawn a huge, excited football crowd. Blue, red and white trappings dotted the stands. And the Giants and Colts players

stirred up enthusiasm during the game. It was a dramatic play-by-play as the New Yorkers defeated the <u>un</u>defeated galloping Colts (known as the "Hosses") 24-21. For that game, the largest number of Giants fans ever had crammed into the stadium. A total of 71,163 howling enthusiasts were there for the upset-win.

"In practice or in a game, Mel Triplett is one of the hardest workers on the Giants team. Football is his trade, and he attacks it with a fervor."[3] And that's what Mel did against Baltimore. He coordinated his efforts with those of Conerly, Gifford, Webster, and Kyle Rote. Together, the high-powered foursome vaulted the Giants into a first-place tie with Cleveland in the Eastern Conference.

<u>Pittsburgh</u>. It was a see-saw season. With a disappointing loss to the Pittsburgh Steelers the following week, the Giants fell back into second place in the Conference. They were looking ahead for their game with Washington, though. They were still positive about making the season finale with the Browns a title game. They were even more certain of their chances with the return of Alex Webster, Jack Stroud, and Roosevelt Brown. That trio had "sat out" with minor injuries during the Pittsburgh game.

"We didn't have it at Pittsburgh," Coach Howell said. *"Even when we were ahead the players didn't have any fire in their eyes. We just couldn't maintain the level we reached against Baltimore and Cleveland....But that's behind us, now we have to work real hard to get back to the spot we were in. Despite our poor showing against the Steelers, the situation is far from hope-less."*[4]

<u>Redskins</u>. So New York's biggest concern was to get ready for Washington. They faced the Redskins in the next game at Yankee Stadium.

Coach Howell was hoping to have a potent offense against the Skins. He needed to coordinate Conerly's aerials to Rote, Gifford, Bob Schnelker. And he needed slants off tackle with power running from Triplett and Webster. If he could match offense and defense, Washington would lose. And he did it. The Giants went ahead that day to win over Washington by 30-0.

<u>Philadelphia</u>. Next week, the Giants scored an important triumph over Philadelphia. They intercepted an Eagles' pass and recovered fumbles. The team from the City of Brotherly Love just couldn't stop the Giants that day. Like Coach Howell said, *"We won because we were able to come up with the big play at the right time. When a big play was needed on attack, our offense came up with it. And when we needed a big play to stop them, our defense came up with it."*[5]

The Giants trail Cleveland by one game in the Eastern Conference. By defeating Philadelphia, though, they were able to keep pace with Cleveland in the conference. Sam Huff led the first-half defensive charge. He blocked what should have been an easy 28-yard field goal by Bobby Walston. Heinrich marched the Giants 60 yards, passing to Schnelker three different times. His final toss was for a touchdown and a 17-10 advantage. On their next series of plays, Gifford and Triplett ran right through the Eagles' defense. They set up Heinrich's scoring pass to Rote. End of tally: 24-10, and two more games to go in the season.

<u>Down to the wire</u>.

Everybody knows it: 1958 was a time in American history crowded with suspense and excitement. The U. S. Army shot America's first satellite, Explorer I, into orbit around the earth. Explorer I inaugurated the Space Age. President Eisenhower sent the U. S. Marines into Lebanon. It was our first military involvement since the Korean War. And the Football Giants, like the New York Yankees, gave fans an adrenalin-pumping year of emotional football.

<u>Cleveland</u>. The Giants had gained "second-life" with a come-from-behind, tightly fought victory over the Detroit Lions. They came to the season finale just one game behind Cleveland. Yankee Stadium was bitterly cold that day. The Giants had home field advantage on a gridiron covered with snow and ice.

Wellington Mara, Giant's owner, took a look at the conditions and felt that the extremely inclement weather might turn the game one way or another on just a break or two.[6]

But snow and ice didn't bother Jim Brown. On the Brown's first series of plays, he took a hand-off from Milt Plum. He got

31

away from Sam Huff. And he galloped 65 yards for a touchdown. Snow and ice? No problem for Jim Brown.

Pat Summerall booted a second period Giants' field goal to make it 7-3. But later, Lou Groza came on to match it and give Cleveland a 10-3 half-time lead. In the third period, New York got a break. Milt Plum fumbled on Cleveland's own 25-yard line and Andy Robustelli recovered it. Then the Giants moved quickly to the 6-yard line on Frank Gifford's pass to Rote. And on the <u>next</u> play, Gifford found Bob Schnelker with a pass. Schnelker "button-hooked" into the end zone for a touchdown and a 10-10 tie.

With just two minutes remaining, Conerly exhausted three downs on three incompleted pass plays. It was fourth down. A punt would end the game in a tie. And a tie wouldn't do New York any good. The chance of going ten yards for the first down on a run or pass play seemed utterly impossible in the inclement weather. Then, to everybody's alarm, Coach Howell called on Pat Summerall to attempt a field goal. Summerall, inspired by all the excitement, booted an amazing 49-yard field goal. It had seemed impossible with the windy field and swirling snow. The Giants won 13-10. Conference play-off was dead ahead.

<u>Road to glory</u>.

The two teams had a week to get ready for the big title game. They tossed a coin to determine who would have home field advantage, and New York won. Play would resume at Yankee Stadium. Very little snow was on the field for this game, but the bitter cold had not diminished. The playing field remained frozen.

Paul Brown, Cleveland's head coach, adjusted his team's game strategy. They shifted from a run- to a pass-oriented offense. Would this cost Cleveland the winning edge? Jim Brown had rushed for 148 yards on 26 tries in the previous game. Also he'd scored an electrifying touchdown run.

<u>Browns again</u>. On game day, the Giants' defense rose to the occasion. They became a cohesive force, like a stone wall, stopping Jim Brown and the Cleveland offense. Brown played his worst game of the season: he made only 8 yards rushing on

7 tries. And the Browns' offense ran just 40 plays the entire afternoon. In contrast, the Giants recorded 80 plays on offense. In this game, the Giants did all the scoring. And a really unusual thing happened. After Charley Conerly marched New York to Cleveland's 19, he incorporated a Vince Lombardi-designed special play.

Conerly took the snap from center Ray Wietecha. Then he handed off to Webster. On a double reverse, Webster gave the ball to Gifford. Next, Gifford sped past the line of scrimmage to about Cleveland's 7-yard line. Suddenly, with a host of Browns tacklers around him, Gifford <u>lateraled</u> the ball back to Charley Conerly. And Conerly raced in for the score.

"That double reverse didn't surprise me," Paul Brown said after the game. *"But the lateral to Conerly? That couldn't have been planned. What the hell was he doing there?"*[7]

Conerly was excited! *"I don't know when I scored last. But it was great for an old guy like me to run it in."* Conerly also said that it was not a fluke. *"The lateral was an option. Vinnie [Lombardi] came up with the play just for this game."*[8]

Pat Summerall's second-quarter field goal was the only other score in the game. And that's how the 1958 Giants won the Eastern Conference Championship, 10-0.

Paul Brown commented on those "invincible" Giants after the game: *"We were surely defeated by a team that was in an inspired state of mind, that's all."*[9]

Ejected after a fight in the second period, Mel Triplett had had "a rough day." He explained the reasons: *"Number 86 [Paul Wiggin] kicked me, and Don Colo grabbed the bar on my mask. That's when we started to go at it. But the officials ought to know it takes two to make a fight."* That time, apparently, it took three.

<u>Next stop, championship?</u>

So the Giants would play for the NFL Championship. It would be their 10th appearance since the annual event was inaugurated in 1933. Weeb Ewbank evaluated the Giants after their win over Cleveland: *"They're a great team. I've never seen a team with as much desire. We'll have to play our best game of the year to win."*[10]

Ewbank's appraisal couldn't have been said any better by any of the other football experts. In the world championship classic, his Colts, the "Hosses", were Western Conference champs. But they would face the Giants: 1958's team with the will to win.

On Sunday, December 28, 1958, the meeting of these two teams would pit the best offensive team in the NFL against the best defensive team. What was certain? One team would rise as the winner and the other would lose. It turned out to be, up to that point, the longest football game in history.

After the excitement of watching pro football's longest game, the emotional spectators left the stands, emotionally drained. The game made football history as the first "sudden-death" game in the NFL. We're familiar with sudden-death play-offs today. But 1958 was the first time in pro football that <u>the first team to score in overtime</u> got the win.

After fumbling away the first half, the Giants came sizzling back in the third quarter. They overcame a Colts' 14-3 lead. And Conerly performed magnificently. His passing <u>almost</u> lead his team to a victory. Almost. Mel Triplett powered over the Colt's 1-yard line for a Giant's third-period touchdown. Gino Marchetti and Gene "Big Daddy" Lipscomb, however, powerful Colts defenders, stopped a later third-down run by Gifford--just a foot short of the first down.

In the fourth quarter, Conerly needed to complete a 15-yard touchdown toss to Gifford. And with Triplett's blocking, he did it. In scoring the go-ahead touchdown, by the way, Gifford made up for two fumbles earlier. Those fumbles had led to two Baltimore scores. Also in the fourth quarter, Andy Robustelli and Jim Katcavage made two massive sacks. They threw Johnny Unitas, the Colts' all-time star quarterback, for successive big losses. For a while, it looked as if the Giants were going to bring home the winner's bacon after all. Instead, on third down, Gifford's run was just short of a first down, and Chandler punted away to Baltimore. Baltimore took over on its own 14-yard line.

Two minutes were left in the fourth period. The Giants were

ahead by a narrow margin, 17-14. Cool-headed John Unitas went to work on the clock. With only 1:56 minutes left in the game, he completed aerial strikes to Lenny Moore and Ray Berry. All the way down to the Giants' 13-yard line. Seconds continued to tick off the clock. The Giants didn't want to believe it, but Steve Myrah kicked a field goal to tie the score. Seven seconds remained in the game. The score stood 17-17.

So, the new fifth-quarter "sudden-death" rule went into effect. The game went into overtime. Fans were going crazy. Everybody was standing up -- or jumping, hollering. Eight minutes and 15 seconds later, the game ended.

The Colts began on the 20 and marched 80 yards down the field in thirteen plays. At the 1-yard line, Unitas handed off to Ameche. Baltimore's great fullback, Allen "The Horse" Ameche, slammed over the Giant's 1-yard line for the touchdown. It was his second of the day. Ameche became an instant hero! The Colts scored the winning touchdown, and suddenly the game was over.

It seemed fitting that the New York <u>Times</u> resumed publication on a downbeat. It headlined Monday's paper with the results of Sunday's gridiron battle. Everything in New York seemed to be diminished. The New York <u>Times</u> front page that Monday said:

TIME AND FORTUNE FINALLY RAN OUT ON PROFES-SIONAL FOOTBALL'S CINDERELLA TEAM, THE NEW YORK GIANTS, AT YANKEE STADIUM[1]

With their 23-17 victory, the Colts won the 1958 NFL Championship. At that time, the game ranked as the most dramatic encounter ever seen in pro football. Bert Bell, NFL commissioner, said, *"It was the greatest game I've ever seen."* Many other football enthusiasts echoed his opinion.

No person's, no football player's personal sacrifices can compare to events that change the lives of nations. But sometimes it's good to look back at "forks in the road," those times that changed the direction of personal lives. Mel Triplett sacrificed part of his potential as a fullback in 1958. It changed the direction of the rest of his life.

He scored a touchdown in the championship game, but only

one during the regular season. Instead, he blocked for team comrades Conerly, Gifford, and Webster. Still, in 1958, he was a team "set up" player: making things happen for other players.

Professional football is "Big Time," and Triplett made his mark in it. Eventually Mel's family, his heart, and much of his career, however, would return to Ohio. He came out of a smoky factory town in Ohio's Steel Valley. He created a legacy in personal standards of achievement for later Steel Valley high school players.

Somebody to look up to. If Mel Triplett could grasp fame and fortune out of the steel towns, maybe they could, too. He left them an example of a championship player who could sacrifice himself for a greater goal: the success of friends, a team, something bigger than himself.

TELEVISION SAW IT

The Giants started their 1959 campaign without their founder, Tim Mara, who died earlier that year. Mara played a significant role in the development of professional football. He was a charter member of the Pro Football Hall of Fame when it opened in 1963.

Mara's life-long goal was to give New York top-quality professional football. He wanted to leave a tradition for his two sons, Jack and Wellington, to carry on in a great American sport. While he was the top executive of the New York Football Giants (34 years), they captured three NFL championships and won eight conference titles.

Allie Sherman, who organized the T-formation for the Giants some years earlier, arrived in 1959 as their new offensive coach. He counted on the Giants' powerful backfield-- Conerly, Gifford, Triplett, and Webster. Sherman's only worry about the backfield was Conerly, starting as quarterback at age 38. Sherman wondered whether or not Conerly could lead his offense in difficult situations: "championship-style."

The defense was no worry. It was its powerful self, with Huff, Robustelli, Katcavage, Grier, Modzelewski, et al. Vince Lombardi remarked before moving to Green Bay, *"Any team that hopes to get by in this conference somehow has to figure how to get past New York's defense. It may be the best in the history of the game."*[1]

<u>All aboard</u>.

Any questions about the offense were answered in the New Yorkers' season opener at Los Angeles. With great blocking from Triplett, Conerly the old "river boat gambler" started a passing attack, and the Giants moved in front for a tightly fought victory.

<u>Philadelphia</u>. Then, in their home opener at Yankee Stadium, they beat the Eagles before a rowdy bunch of fans. All the Giants' talented performers played heads-up ball that day, avenging a 49-21 set-back by the Eagles two weeks earlier. Allie Sherman's man-in-motion attack was a success story for the New York offense. Conerly, Gifford, Triplett, and Webster car-

37

ried out the play formations almost flawlessly.

Tom Landry's well-disciplined defensive squad also featured in New York's win over the City of Brotherly Love.

The man-in-motion play was a pillar of strength for the New York team. It threw Philadelphia's defensive line out of adjustment. The following play sketch illustrates the man-in-motion with blocking assignments, Webster as the ball carrier.

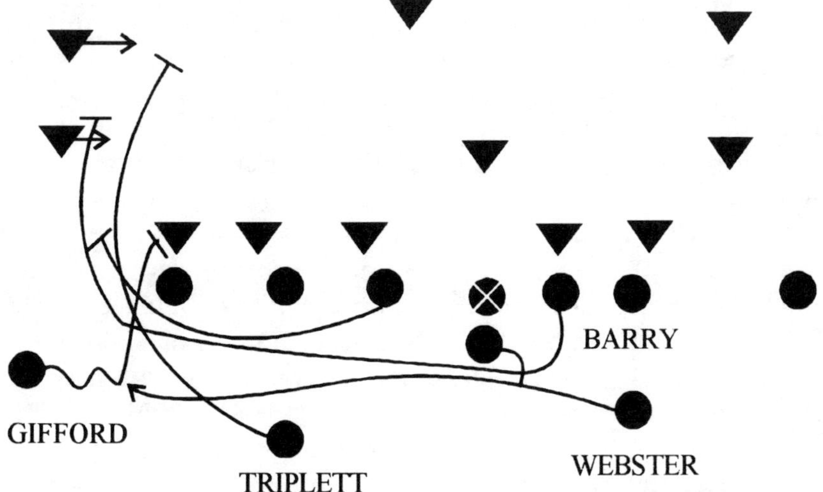

Figure 2

In previous encounters, New York had always used the motion man as a pass receiver, ball carrier, or as a decoy. Never entirely as a blocker. When used as a lead blocker, the man-in-motion opened the outside path around Philadelphia's right defensive end. The Giants then made a second-period touchdown. With the new option, New York could use a variety of plays on the motion side of the field, either left or right.

Alex Webster and Frank Gifford shared the man-in-motion responsibility, Gifford from the left side and Webster from the right. Gifford was the motion-man when Webster raced 16 yards for New York's second touchdown in the Philadelphia game.

Before Conerly took the snap from Wietecha, Gifford started to run. He looked to be headed from his wide flanking position toward New York's left end. On the snap, Gif angled toward the left. On the angle, Gifford exploded into the Eagles' right line-backer--tying him up with a solid shoulder block. Webster swept left and went in for the score.

While Gifford was throwing his block, so was Mel Triplett. He had an important role--to knock down the Eagles' corner man or defensive back. And to help clear the way for Webster when he took Conerly's hand-off. Allie Sherman explained, *"Mel Triplett then went to fill the gap in the Eagles backfield and Al Barry and Darrell Dess, our guards, led the way downfield for Webster."*[2]

Gifford didn't mind his new role as a blocker. Sherman said, *"It's tough to have a 200-pound halfback run in to block a 230-pound or 240-pound linebacker. But when Gifford hit him this way, the linebacker wasn't expecting him and that made it easy for Frank."*[3]

Triplett worked hard at his blocking, too, in practice or in games. He took on the tasks as a matter of pride, of self-satisfaction. He had enormous power for a man weighing only 215-pounds. But it was normal for Trip to uncoil and knock a 240-pound lineman flat.

<u>Halfway home</u>.

The Giants bested Green Bay 20-3 at Yankee Stadium. Triplett and Stroud cleared the way, throwing some great blocks for Webster. Webster scored two touchdowns on New York's pet play called "28 Sweep." It was a bread-and-butter play for New York throughout the season.

Against Green Bay, New York's <u>entire</u> defense hit about as hard as Triplett did on one of his ferocious blocks. The Giants' defense simply hit harder, rushed harder, and tackled harder than Green Bay's. Robustelli, Huff, Svare, Modzelewski, Livingston, and Grier all played great defensive football that day.

The Giants' defense also had pet names for special defensive plays. One was called "Blitz Wanda." "Storm Sarah" was another.

"Red Dog Meg," was another. Whoever designed these plays created them to <u>attack</u> the passer or <u>intimidate</u> the ball carrier.

Harland Svare explained in the locker room, after the game, why "Blitz Wanda" and "Storm Sarah" were used as call names for two of the Giants' defensive plays. *"We couldn't find another girl's name that begins with W to designate the weak side linebacker. 'Storm Sarah,'"* he added, *"is the term used when the Giants' strong-side linebacker is the blitzer."*[4]

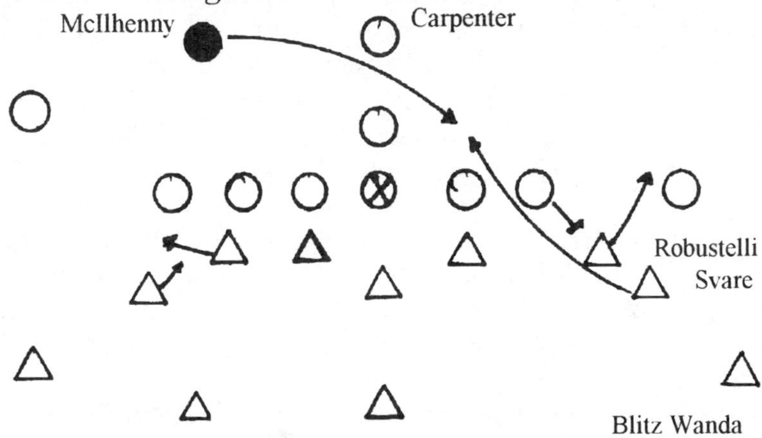

Without great blockers, the offense does not move, as we all know. Blockers are just as important as outstanding defensive men. Triplett, of course, was one of New York's most ferocious blockers and one of the greatest that ever played in the NFL. Conerly wasn't the only one who reaped glory from Triplett's great blocking. New York's "Golden Boys"--Gifford and Webster-- raced for most of their touchdowns off Trip's bruising blocks.

Frank Gifford once spoke about Mel's blocking ability. *"He doesn't just block 'em, either,"* he said, smiling with admiration, *"...he flattens 'em."*[5]

<u>Washington</u>. As the 1959 season moved along, Triplett continued with power and consistency to run and block for the Giants' offense. He helped his team to a spectacular win over the Washington Redskins. Shivering and excited, the fans came to Yankee Stadium on November 29th to watch New York rout the Redskins 45-14. Conerly, with plenty of time to pass, threw three touchdown tosses, leading New York to victory.

It was also a special day for quarterback Conerly. Officials had declared it "Charley Conerly Day" at Yankee Stadium, giving him special praise and honors before the game started. Charley played superb football that day, hard to do under the holiday circumstances.

Webster scored the first touchdown of the game--a 10-yard run on New York's famous "28 Sweep" play. Everything about New York's play was outstanding. Gifford, Triplett, King, and Webster -- all four had a fine day with their rushing yardage.

Cleveland. The most important game of the season wrapped up the Giants' third Eastern Conference championship in four years. No surprise at the outcome: the Giants defeated the Browns. But the Giants did astonish a bellowing horde of fanatic fans with the trouncing they gave Cleveland in Yankee Stadium.

Near the end of the game, New York fans turned rowdy, and a jubilant mob went on a 20-minute siege of the playing field. They ripped down one goal post and were heading for the other end zone. It took all available policemen and an appeal from the Giants players to restore order. Only 113 seconds remained on the game clock. Fights broke out everywhere in the crowd. It was an all-out effort for police to keep up with the hullabaloo.

Cleveland's only touchdown came in the fourth quarter, after trailing 48-0. Head coach Paul Brown unhappily gave his account of the match up. *"We did not belong on the same field with them today,"* he said at the end.[5]

But the key to Conerly's success lay with the amazing protection he got from his blockers. Even the Browns' defensive linemen made comments.

"We couldn't get to Conerly," was the complaint of the Cleveland linemen. "Conerly had perfect protection," some said. "The blocking for Conerly was excellent,"[6] others added.

Miles away and like the New York fans, Baltimore Colts fans were in a happy hysteria, too. The Colts had won the Western Conference championship. Thus, the Colts and Giants would match up for the second year in a row, playing for the NFL championship at Baltimore's Memorial Stadium.

Baltimore. Big Johnny Unitas was a standout performer for the Colts in that championship game on December 27, 1959. He passed for two touchdowns and ran for one himself. Earlier in his career, the Pittsburgh Steelers had released Unitas. He hitchhiked home to Pittsburgh. All he got was $6-a-game as a semi-pro player with the Bloomfield Rams before he joined the

Colts. Afterward, <u>Sport Magazine</u> chose him as the championship game's most valuable player.

Baltimore also had defensive stars such as Gino Marchetti, Bill Pellington, Don Shinnick, and Art Donovan. They thwarted the Giants' offense in key situations. The New Yorkers' T-attack offense lacked zeal. It seemed lackadaisical, especially the offensive line blocking.

Even so, the Giants still had a 9-7 lead late in the third period. Then came the turning point for Baltimore. On fourth down, New York had the ball on the Colts' 28-yard line with inches to go for a first down. Webster took a hand-off from Conerly and hit hard into the Colts defensive line but was hammered back, still <u>inches short</u> of the first down.

Things might have been different for New York if Webster had made that first down. Instead, the Colts gained momentum and went on to dismantle the Giants in a 31-16 triumph. It was Baltimore's second straight world championship against a great New York club. Coach Ewbank of the Colts, in the locker room after Baltimore's victory, proclaimed: *"Once the snowball started rolling, there was no stopping it."*[7]

"Holding them to less than a yard was the key to the switch,"[8] said Ewbank about Webster's not making the first down. Coach Ewbank had great respect for the Giants, too. *"That was a great team we beat,"* he said, *"and we feel happy and fortunate that the fellow upstairs was smiling on us."*[9]

<u>After the shouting...</u>

The Good Lord had special purposes for Mel Triplett all along his journey through life. From the Mississippi Delta, farming cotton, Mel moved to the steel-mill town of Girard, Ohio, thence to Toledo University. From Toledo, he moved to the New York Giants. Rivals of the Giants wanted to put the quarterback from Ole Miss, Charley Conerly, out of action. Somehow, though, they couldn't do it. The <u>reason</u> for their lack of success was big #33--Mel Triplett.

In his first five years as a Giant, Triplett was "Chuckin'" Charlie's personal bodyguard on the gridiron. Whenever Conerly dropped back to pass, Triplett set up a one-man roadblock. He just dared opposing defensive men to get past him.

Some did, of course. But most who did suffered lumps and bruises. They all believed Triplett was one of the greatest blockers ever to play pro football. Triplett meant to Conerly what Allen Ameche meant to Johnny Unitas. What Marion Motley meant to Otto Graham: <u>protection</u>.

"It makes you feel kinda good to know that Triplett is up there blocking for you,"[10] Conerly once said. He admitted that Mel's protective measures were key reasons for his aerial success.

When Trip wasn't blocking or scoring for the Giants, he was back home with his wife Gladys and their children. He was a traditional family man. He learned old-fashioned American values from growing up in a very large family.

Trip was a hero not only on the field but off the field, also. Overcoming a limited educational background, he worked 40-hour weeks during high school and college to support his family: completed his college education; and earned honors in sports at all levels. The obstacles he faced and the successes he won are prime models of determination and perseverance.

In his five years with the Giants, Mel played on one world championship team (1956) and three Eastern Conference championship teams (1956, 1958 and 1959) of the National Football League.

*Mel Triplett - Courtesy of Minnesota Football Vikings
and the New York Football Giants.*

TRADES AND FADES

The year 1960 ushered in an era in television coverage of pro football that focused on single players. Special TV documentaries spotlighted certain star talents and their specific roles. For example, one program featured Sam Huff of the Giants, the "father of middle linebackers," as a key defensive figure. It gave a step-by-step description of his particular job.

This kind of TV coverage showed the importance of the middle linebacker. It made a Sunday afternoon hero of the middleman as he picked up most of the tackling assignments. Likewise, players on offense got special attention when the time was right. Some individual Giants got their share on opening day of the regular season.

Off to the races.

During the first game that fall, George Shaw replaced Charlie Conerly in the second half. Shaw lead the New Yorkers to a come-from-behind win over the 49ers in San Francisco that day.

Mel Triplett aided the offense with a third period touchdown run. And scored again in the fourth quarter on a 24-yard toss from Shaw.

San Francisco's quarterback had engineered a couple of drives that put the 49ers on the score board. He tossed passes to Monty Stickles and Hugh McElhenny. Tittle and McElhenny seemed to be invincible on the screen-pass play, time and time again. But the Giants' defense stopped San Francisco inches short of a fourth-quarter winning touchdown. The heroes of that great goal-line stand were Katcavage, Huff, and Robustelli.

According to Conerly, when the Giants won, he was upgraded to "old pro" status. But when the club lost, he was demoted to "old man"[1] category. Unfortunately that day, Conerly set up the 49ers' first touchdown by fumbling on his first passing attempt.

St. Louis. The following week at Busch Stadium, the Giants' offense was sluggish during most of the first half. But once the

New Yorkers really began to play, they rolled to a 35-14 victory. It was the Cardinals' first game after moving from Chicago. This was also the game in which somebody called big #33 "the Triplett of old." Of "old"? That description came after Trip galloped 33 yards for a touchdown on a quick opener.

The Cards posed a problem to the Giants' defense. It was difficult to stop Frank "Pop" Ivy's squad. Their offense ran the imaginative "double-wing-T" formation, several players handling the ball on many plays. The Giants' defense, however, had the will to win. They proved it <u>could</u> be done.

<u>Unbeatable?</u>

In their home opener at Yankee Stadium, the New Yorkers battled the Washington Redskins to a 24-24 tie. Mayor Wagner and New York City officials had declared the entire game-week "New York Football Giants Week." After such publicity, the Giants did everything possible to make a good showing.

The following week, however, against the St. Louis Cardinals once more, the Giants tasted the bitterness of defeat. They lost by a score of 20-13, the result of three fumbles and five interceptions. Like they say, "Aside from that, Mrs. Lincoln, how did you enjoy the play?" You might say that <u>aside from the turnovers</u>. Tripplett enjoyed a good game. He led the ground attack in the second period and scored a touchdown. But for the team it was a somber day.

<u>Cleveland</u>. Before a record crowd the following week, the Giants played the Browns at Municipal Stadium. Every fan was aware that the Giants played a resourceful ballgame that day. Many of the millions who saw it on television agreed.

It was a cold day for football as a sharp breeze blew in from Lake Erie. But the New York defense got down to business right away. It contained powerful Jim Brown and elusive Bobby Mitchell all afternoon.

Conerly was back at quarterback for New York. He engineered the scoring surges. Gifford and Triplett each capped the ground gains with a touchdown run. Pat Summerall added a field goal. At the half, the Giants had a 10-6 lead. But at the start of the third quarter, Cleveland regained the point advantage. Ray Renfro, a Cleveland flanker, caught a touchdown pass from

Milt Plum. Once again, it was "back to the drawing board."

So Conerly led New York on an 80-yard drive. Gifford ran into the end zone for the final six yards and ended the scoring. Gifford and Triplett were the game's top ground gainers. Powerful, bruising Triplett plowed through Cleveland's defense for 137 yards, and Gifford piled up another 71. They easily out-rushed their counterparts, Jim Brown and Bobby Mitchell.

<u>Tally time</u>.

With their win, they had won a really unexpected, upset victory. It was a monumental achievement in their sixth straight defeat of the Browns. Thus, the Giants were back in the Eastern Conference title race and appeared to be <u>the</u> team to be reckoned with. Triplett was the game's top rusher. And their defense had held Cleveland's powerful offense to just 6 rushing yards all afternoon.

<u>Pittsburgh</u>. Most of the fans at Yankee Stadium the next week had doubts about New York's chances of winning. The game started badly for the Giants. Quickly, the Steelers scored first. Then, Triplett fumbled in the first period, giving the Steelers possession again. A few minutes later, Bobby Layne marched his club into the end zone for a score and a 14-0 advantage.

But the Giants still had a great attacking unit with Conerly, Gifford, Triplett, and Bobby Simms only to come back and squeak-out a fourth quarter triumph.

<u>Countdown</u>.

As the campaign wound down during its final weeks, the Giants lost two, won one, and tied one. They finished third behind second-place Cleveland in the Eastern Conference.

Tom Landry's Dallas Cowboys captured a moral victory in their game against the Giants. They played New York to a 31-31 tie. Moral victory or not, Triplett gave the Giants the advantage when he made the game's first touchdown. It came on a 10-yard toss from Shaw. Joe Morrison went in for a second tally from the 1-yard line, after a Shaw pass to Kyle Rote. So, the Giants did get off to a fast start. But the Cowboys matched them point-for-point.

With the suggestion of a smile, Tom Landry accepted

congratulations after the game. *"Half a loaf is better than nothing, I guess," he said. "I'm proud of my team for the way it stuck in there."*[3]

The season finale again was against arch-rival Cleveland. In the second quarter, Mel picked up most of his game total 72 yards. He led a stampede through the Browns' defense. The Giants moved 75 yards, and Pat Summerall kicked a 12-yard field goal. Later, however, Mel could play only as a blocker. He reinjured his left hand when he returned the second-half kick-off. Even so, he was the Giants' top ground gainer for the day. The whole team played their hearts out that day: their head coach, Jim Lee Howell, was retiring.

Still, Cleveland won the right to play in the League's first runner-up bowl game. The Browns demystified the Giants' mystique by winning 48-34. And, reluctantly, the Giants' dynasty came to an end. The Giants had started showing their age: one-fourth of the players were 30 years old or older. Wellington Mara, team owner, wanted to rebuild the Giants. He hoped to get Vince Lombardi as the team's new head coach. But Lombardi could not break his contract with the Green Bay Packers and had to refuse Mara's offer.

End of an era. Howell retired to the Giants' front office. He had compiled a record of 53 wins, 27 losses, and 4 ties. In seven years as head coach, he had won three conference titles and one world championship.

The Giants finished in third place in the Eastern Conference of the NFL that year. Still, their defense repeated as the best in the league against the run. They allowed their opponents only 3.2 yards per carry, a slightly better average than their 1959 record. Coach Howell was also proud of the fact that the Giants were the best team on defense against passing, along with San Francisco. They allowed opponents to complete only 47.8 percent of their passes. In that rating, New York finished in front of Baltimore, Philadelphia, Detroit, Los Angeles, and Dallas.

According to the football world, the Giants' defense established itself as one of the greatest in the history of professional football. Any one could understand why--with a line-up of titans like Andy Robustelli, Rosy Grier, Sam Huff, Jim Patton, and

Dick "Little Mo" Modzelewski. Yes, the Giants had stars on defense and, quite likely, the greatest defensive record of all time. Likewise, they had stars on offense: Charlie Conerly, Frank Gifford, Rosy Brown, Kyle Rote, and Mel Triplett--their 1960 top ground-gainer.

In addition to Triplett's reputation as a great blocker, he was also a superior runner. In his last season with the Giants, he ground out 573 yards on 122 attempts as a power-rusher, with a 4.6 average, to become the clubs top ground gainer. When he left the Giants, he was the 5th leading rusher in Giants' history. And he ranked 9th in the entire NFL.

During six seasons with the Giants, #33 carried the ball 551 times for 2,298 yards, a 4.2-yard average per rush. Also, he scored 14 touchdowns. Add 368 yards for pass receptions to his 2,298 rushing yards: that makes his total yardage 2,666. Those are remarkable six-year totals for a blocking back.

<u>Goodbye, New York</u>.

Yes, in 1961 he left the Giants. The Giants traded Triplett to the Minnesota Vikings (along with Bob Schnelker and Bob Schmidt) for two draft picks--Zeke Smith and Dave Whitsell.

The Vikings picked up one of the NFL's top fullbacks when they obtained Triplett from the Giants. Big, powerful Triplett kept his jersey number (33) and joined the backfield ranks of Fran Tarkenton, Tommy Mason, and Hugh McElhenny. The Vikings knew of Triplett's real forte as a blocker as well as his running ability. They knew very well that he was one of the best blockers in the game.

<u>Injuries...injuries</u>. The 1962 campaign, however, was less productive. Suffering from a knee injury, Mel was able to carry the ball only 52 times. His carries totaled only 160 yards, a 3.1-yard average. And he scored only two touchdowns. When looking at their future plans, the Vikings decided to try out three younger fullbacks in Mel's place. After he sat out for a month, somebody asked Mel about the younger competition. *"I think,"* said Triplett, *"that I'm the best fullback on this club, on experience and what I can do for it."*[4]

Triplett fielded another question about his ability as a

player. *"I've been in this league for seven years. Nobody has ever said I couldn't play a full season. I'll block for the passer. when it's third down and we've got to get the ball away. I'll run to the outside or inside, wherever they ask me....All I ever wanted is a chance to run the ball when it will help the club. The Vikings gave me the chance last year. I ran for them."*[5]

Meanwhile, the Vikings finally decided that Triplett did not fit into their plans. They traded him to the Cleveland Browns at the close of the 1962 season. Asked about the trade:

"The Vikings," Trip replied, *"know what they're doing. and they know what I can do. They are more interested in the younger guys. That's okay with me. I was always willing to be judged by what I could do out there. I do the best I can. and I hope it's good enough. When I don't think I can help anybody. I'll stop coming to camp."*[6]

The following summer (1963), Triplett entered the Cleveland Browns' training camp, hoping to become Jim Brown's running mate in the 1963 season. After watching the ex-Giant fullback two days, head coach Blanton Collier wasn't counting him <u>out</u> at the slot.

Mel, 32 years old at the time, worked hard. That age is right on the verge of "over the hill" for professional football players. Yet he blasted away in those early training camp sessions at Hiram College. And he felt fully recuperated from the previous season's knee injury. During training camp, a reporter asked Trip why he played so well against the Browns during his years with the Giants.

"We all considered that a bread-and-butter game," he explained. *"Championship money usually was on the line. Beating the Browns was like winning two games."*[7]

"We know that Triplett can block and is a hard runner." Collier answered later. But the Browns gave Trip his final release--just two days before the squad left for a series of West Coast exhibition games. One of the best ground-gainers for eight pro seasons had reached the end of his football career.[8]

LITTLE BROTHER GROWS UP

Bill Triplett followed in Mel's footsteps. He was a star halfback-fullback for Girard High from 1955-57. In developing his SVC football traditions, Bill was elusive and fast. He helped Girard High win its 1955 conference co-championship with Campbell Memorial High.

Each school took a share of the prestigious Ingot Award Trophy, presented to the SVC championship-team each year by WBBW Radio. Al Mauriocourt (Girard) and Johnny Knapick (Campbell Memorial) were the head coaches. Both were pleased and honored with their teams' accomplishments in such a highly competitive conference.

Before attending Girard, Bill (like his brother) was born on a Mississippi cotton farm. He didn't develop his physical strength by plowing furrows with a team of mules. He did, however, possess about the same power and athletic ability when he entered high school. He just had a different _style_ of running.

While in junior high school and through Mel's influence, Bill became interested in football. Under Coach Mauriocourt's training, he became one of the greatest running backs ever to play in the SVC. He attained both All-SVC and All-Ohio honors. After his senior year, he received offers from several colleges and universities around the country to play football. Bill wanted, however, to stay close to home. So he accepted a football scholarship from Miami (Ohio) University.

At Miami, Bill was a three-year letterman and, in his senior year, captain of the football team. He set records at Miami as an all-around athlete. Also, he was an All-Mid American Conference selection. Bill was the first Miami player ever to play in the East-West Shrine game. And he played in the Hula Bowl that year, too.

St. Louis rookie.

After earning such an outstanding college record, Bill was 6th in the 1962 pro-football draft. The New York Giants drafted him, then traded him to the St. Louis Cardinals. In turn, the Cardinals had traded quarterback Ralph Guglielmi for Triplett plus a high draft choice.

Coach Wally Lemm and talent scout Abe Stuber had seen fullback Bill Triplett in action. They were encouraged by his abilities and potential as a future pro. *"I'm sure Triplett can help us,"*[1] said Lemm, who spent several days that week at staff meetings with his new coaches Fran Polsfoot and Don Shroyer. *"Bill is strong and fast and, besides being a good fullback, he also is a fine defensive player."*[2]

A former Notre Dame All-American, Guglielmi had started playing for the Washington Redskins in 1955. He was their first-string quarterback before the Redskins traded him to the Cardinals. Then, Guglielmi went from the Cardinals to the Giants--to fill the spot created by Charlie Conerly's retirement. By acquiring Triplett, the Cardinals had added strength at the fullback position. They had missed several chances to draft their first-choice picks. They also expected their young quarterback, Charlie Johnson, to back up Sam Etcheverry.

"We didn't figure we could carry three quarterbacks, none of whom could double up by playing defense, especially if Jerry Norton goes through with his plans to retire."[3] Lemm explained.

The Big Red wanted to draft All-American Bob Ferguson of Ohio State. A last minute decision, though, gave the Pittsburgh Steelers first chance, and Pittsburgh chose Ferguson. Bob Jackson of New Mexico State also was a third-round selection by St. Louis. But he joined the San Diego Chargers of the American Football League. Thus, St. Louis acquired Bill Triplett from the Giants. He would be competing against Frank Mestnik and Mal Hammak for the fullback position.

More important: Bill could double as a defensive back. In a September exhibition game against the Detroit Lions, Bill proved his ability. He played in the Cards' defensive backfield, and the coaches evaluated how he played. Coach Lemm remarked, *"We had Bill Triplett in there just a short time, and he showed us he could tackle and had potential as a defensive back."*[4]

The Big Red was short of defensive backs. As a result, after film-and practice-evaluations, Lemm decided to give Trip a first-string position in the secondary. Bill learned his duties quickly. He teamed with star players such as Jimmy Hill and Larry Wilson. Triplett would much rather have run the ball instead of chasing it on defense. But, first of all, he wanted to do what was needed to help the club.

<u>Dallas</u>. St. Louis (2-4-1) was not having a great year. Even so, Triplett did his part in the Big Red's 28-24 triumph over the Dallas Cowboys. The Cards played a "read the keys" defense against the Cowboys' shifty, jumping-Jack offense. On the field 38 minutes, the Cards' defensive squad was the most important factor in the win. They had to battle against 73 Dallas offensive plays.

On offense, Charlie Johnson threw three touchdown passes, two to Sonny Randle. Those scores gave the Cardinals a winning edge. But the defense was responsible for their fourth-quarter victory touchdown. Bill Stacy jarred the ball loose from Cowboy Don Meredith, and Bill Koman recovered.

That game was the Cards' first win since opening day. Their performance set a positive tone for the remaining half of the season. But Tom Landry's multiple-attack offense was tough to stop. With its hard runners, fine passers, and excellent receivers, the Cowboys could pull an upset victory over any club in the East.

Coach Lemm prepared his defensive strategy with a reversed secondary. Stacy would play on the flanker side of the field to cover Dallas's fast receivers. Rookie Triplett would play a safety spot along with Wilson. Lemm's set-up overcame a weakness in the Cardinals defense.

"We had Triplett and Wilson reversing positions, so that Wilson was always the free safety man and Triplett always was on the tight-end side of the Dallas formation.' Lemm said. *"It gave Triplett a lot less to learn in preparing for the game."*[5]

<u>San Francisco</u>. Triplett came a long way as a pro football player after the beginning of the season. He worked hard at it every day. He was living a dream he'd had for years. From the time he left Walnut Street in Girard to play for the Miami Redskins, he'd wanted to play <u>pro</u> football.

The Cards were having a losing year, that's true. But Trip

battled alongside his defensive teammates <u>trying</u> to win. Tough luck: the San Francisco 49ers won at Busch Stadium. They made touchdowns from Cardinal errors --intercepted two Cardinal passes and recovered a Big Red fumble. Also, the Cards lost a third-quarter touchdown on a penalty call-back.

Quarterback Brodie remarked in the San Francisco locker room afterward, *"They [the Cards] sure put on a pass rush. They shoot everybody through at you but the housekeeper."*[6]

Red Hickey, the 49er's head coach, commented on the Big Red defense. *"St. Louis is tough to move against, and that blitz by the Cardinals is well organized. This time the breaks came our way."*[7] The 49ers won, 24-17.

<u>End of the year</u>. As the season came to a close, St. Louis could muster few positive memories. Mostly, they had to endure the dismal knowledge they'd finished at less than .500. Still, a few wins are better than none. The Cardinal offense had displayed a lot of power. <u>Errors</u> were what prevented their power from posting numbers on the scoreboard. And even at that, Cardinal offensive yardage ranked third in the NFL. On defense, safety Larry Wilson had consistently played good ball. And rookie Triplett had done well, even though he got a late start at the other safety spot.

"Continuing to use the safety blitz, the Cards occasionally made it rough on opposing quarterbacks, but the end result was not sufficient."[8]

"I haven't yet put a finger on what we can do on pass defense." Lemm said. *"I think--and this is hindsight--that if we had gone with Triplett at the start, we'd have been better. He'd have had more experience."*[9]

Individually, Trip returned 24 kickoffs for a total of 608 yards, a 25.3 average. A 49-yarder was his longest. Those were outstanding statistics for a speedster in his first year. As a result of the season's developments, St. Louis had a good nucleus of talent to start the following year.

<u>Seasoned veterans</u>.
When the 1963 campaign opened, Coach Lemm moved Triplett to <u>offense</u>. Trip played right halfback in the Big Red's

standard T-formation in the regular season opener. This time, they opened against the Dallas Cowboys at the Cotton Bowl. The Cardinals used the "T-Formation" (three backs behind the quarterback; both ends split 10-12 yards) in only three offensive series.

But Trip played the whole game. When it was all over, he had rushed for 82 yards in 12 tries. <u>And</u> he had pulled down two passes for 51 yards. He helped the cards to a 34-7 win. Poor Cowboy's fans.

Something took place for Triplett that day even more important than the outstanding plays he had in Dallas. That season-opener was the game in which Bill Triplett was no longer "Mel's little brother." Bill became a full-fledged pro ball-player: <u>himself</u> during the Cardinals' crushing victory over the Cowboys.

Ever since December 1961, Bill had been referred to as "Mel's younger brother." All families know it. Brothers and sisters compete with each other. Some kids resent it. Others don't. During the Dallas game, Bill achieved his own level of excellence, becoming the NFL's second leading rusher. Nobody needed to mention Mel any longer to identify Bill.

His second-place status looms larger when you realize that Jim Brown was in first place. Brown had been the NFL's No. 1 rusher five years in a row while playing for the Cleveland Browns. And so, after the Dallas game, folks mentioned Bill first to identify "Bill's older brother," Mel.

<u>Philadelphia</u>. In front of enthused fans at Franklin Field the next week, Triplett scored the Cards' first touchdown on a 1-yard plunge. That score set the pace for the Cards' 28-24 victory over Philadelphia. With Childress and Triplett hustling in the offense, St. Louis came back twice to overcome 10-point deficits.

<u>Time out!</u>

That same day, an article in the St. Louis paper said:

The U.S. Fourth Circuit Court of Appeals unanimously upheld a lower court decision that had ruled against the American Football League in its $10,800,000 antitrust suit against the National Football League. The AFL promptly appealed the decision"[10]

Just a quick bit of history here for fans who weren't with us in the 1940's or 50's, all right? Back in 1946, an 8-team football league formed as a rival to the NFL. It called itself the All-America Football Conference. The two "leagues" joined forces in 1950, adding three AAFC teams to the NFL. But that merger didn't clear up all the problems.

In 1960, an eight-team professional league began to operate as the American Football League. Fueled by generous contracts from television networks, the two leagues battled fiercely for college talent.[11]

And the competing leagues went to court, as the <u>Dispatch</u> news article said. Finally, in 1966, they settled their differences, forming the NFL we know today—with American and National <u>conferences</u>.

<u>Resume play</u>.

But actually, the next week at Forbes Field, under black clouds and a rising wind, the Pittsburgh Steelers judged St. Louis's mistakes. Their decision? A clear defeat. The Cards couldn't appeal that decision anywhere.

"Our mistakes hurt us." Lemm continued. *"One penalty we incurred prevented a touchdown, another gave us only a field goal instead of a touchdown, another helped Pittsburgh get a touchdown, and a fumble set up another for the Steelers."*[12]

Triplett's first-quarter 63-yard touchdown, however, was all the Cards could muster in the first half. Unfortunately, his game total of 73 yards rushing did not give the strong Cardinal team enough edge. Art Rooney, sportsman-owner of the Steelers, offered a consoling thought. *"The Cardinals are a really strong team—they'll have a shot at it [the division title] yet."*[13]

<u>Vikings</u>. The next week, Triplett's touchdown runs sparked the Cards to a triumph over Minnesota. For the Vikings, it was a dismal game at Metropolitan Stadium before a covenant of subdued fans. With the win, the Cards made a nice comeback from their loss the previous week. But they knew they faced a tough battle in their next game—against Pittsburgh.

<u>Steelers</u>. It was an action-packed game. St. Louis had to

overcome a 13-point fourth-quarter deficit. And they did it. Johnson's fiery aerials defeated the Steelers 24-23. Triplett slashed four yards to Pittsburgh's one-yard line in the first period. That gave the Cards an early scoring opportunity. But they were unable to get the ball into the end zone until later in the game.

Giants. When the eighth game of the campaign ended, the Cards fell back in the Conference. Triplett had rushed 85 yards in 11 tries and scored a fourth-period touchdown. That bolstered the Big Red offensive attack.

Triplett re-bruised his sore shoulder on his touchdown run. Like so many football players do, though, he continued to play while injured.

In another sport, Rocky Colavito had been a powerful hitter eight full seasons in the American League. A former Cleveland Indian right-fielder, he was traded to the Kansas City Athletics from the Detroit Tigers. *"We are paying a heavy price to acquire the power hitting we need."*[14] said Athletic's general manager Pat Friday.

Browns. The Cardinals needed power, too, and they paid a heavy price for victory in their win over the Cleveland Browns. Bruises and injuries can't be measured in dollars and cents, but eventually they collect their dues.

Giants. Depressed football fans gathered in the stands the following week, 48 hours after the assassination of President John F. Kennedy. The NFL was holding to its seven-game schedule under orders from Commissioner Pete Rozelle. Determined protests, of course, came from different sides shaken by the tragedy.

"It was hard to think about football before the game." said Charlie Johnson. *"I really didn't have the sharpness which comes with mental preparation before the game. I am sure it was the same way with the Giants too."* Sam Huff said, *"I feel depressed. I feel as bad about it as anybody."*[15]

But somehow the Cards managed to play a little better than the Giants that day. They won before a fiery group of fans at Yankee Stadium. Tripletts fumble recovery, rushing yardage, and 14-yard touchdown run over right guard paved the way.

But Bill's biggest day of the year (102 yards rushing in 16 tries) came against a real tough Cleveland Browns' defense in game #12. It almost went unnoticed, because the Big Red lost 24-10. Still, it was Trip's first 100-yard day. With that win, the Browns tied for the top spot, once again, with the Giants in the Eastern Conference.

In the season finale, St. Louis dropped to third place by losing to the Dallas Cowboys, 28-24. But overall, it was St. Louis's best campaign finish since 1948. Wilson and Triplett led the Cardinals' ground attack. Each scored a touchdown, to tally most of the Cards' points. Don Meredith connected with Pettis Norman and Frank Clarke for most of the Cowboys' touchdowns and game-winning points.

All in all, Bill Triplett had a great year in 1963. He added up 652 yards in 134 tries, a 4.9 average. He scored five touchdowns on the ground. His longest run of the year was a 63-yard touchdown sprint against the Pittsburgh Steelers.

ERASE THAT YEAR

If Bill Triplett could have, he would have tossed out the whole 1964 football campaign. It was a totally frustrating year. He was stricken by tuberculosis and couldn't play. At all. One Friday evening in March, while sitting at the dinner table, he felt a slight pain in his chest.

When he complained of the pain, his wife, Jacqueline, said, *"Oh. it's probably something you have eaten."*[1] But when the pain recurred the next night, she made a doctor's appointment for Bill the next day.

Triplett had a slight fever, and his family doctor recommended a battery of x-rays. When reading the x-rays, the doctor noticed a dark spot on one of Bill's lungs. He diagnosed the illness immediately as a virulent tubercular bacillus, and he did not hesitate. *"You're a sick man,"* he told Bill. *"You're going right into the hospital."*

"How can I be sick? I don't feel sick, I don't look sick."[2] But Bill was lucky the doctor caught the disease in time, before it disabled him. He was confined to the hospital a few weeks. When Bill was released, the doctor restricted him from playing football. All year.

It was a trying time for Bill, having to sit out the 1964 season. Especially after he'd teamed with such back-field men as John David Crow and Prentice Gautt the year before. But the St. Louis Cardinals gave him a job working in the front office as a public relations consultant for the year.

"We miss you, we miss you real bad,"[3] Coach Lemm said to Triplett one Thursday. It was Bill's first day back since his outstanding performance a year earlier.

He had expected to have an even better season than he'd had the previous year--before being sidelined with illness. He enjoyed talking with Coach Lemm and some of his assistant coaches on that first day. Trip also went out to watch the Cardinals' afternoon practice. They were getting ready for their finale against Washington in the exhibition season.

Of course, Triplett felt enthusiastic and wanted to play the season. Backfield Coach Charlie Trippe said, *"You look ready right now."*[4] Trip was a slim 196 pounds, 14 pounds under his previous year's weight. Coach Lemm patted him on the back and said, *"Bill's going to be back to 215 next year. I know that."*[5] Weight-gain wouldn't be too difficult, because shortly after his doctor put him on medication, Bill had dropped to 175 pounds.

"I was taking 28 pills a day," said Bill, *"and they did not agree with my stomach. My system just couldn't cope with them. In fact, they thought I had pneumonia at first."*[6]

It was the first illness Bill had ever had in his life. He said, *"I felt good during the weeks they had me in the hospital. I feel great now physically and I've always felt that way, although I was depressed when they first told me of my illness."*[7] From that point on, Triplett began an intensive physical conditioning program, retraining himself for the 1965 season.

"After our last game here with Dallas," Bill said, *"I said to myself that 1964 was going to be an even better year for me. I was convinced that I could do better--after being doubtful about my chances as an offensive halfback--before we opened the season against the Cowboys at Dallas."*[8]

Moreover, the Cards' coaching staff felt strongly that, if Bill could have played with the 1964 squad, the Cards could have finished first in the Eastern Conference. As it was, they finished second (9-3-2) behind the first-place Cleveland Browns (10-3-1).

During his training program, Bill became known as the "Comeback Cardinal" of the 1965 campaign. The season actually started in November, 1964 for him. That's when his doctor gave Bill his clearance to start the exercise program.

First, Bill began an exercise routine coupled with jogging short distances. He coordinated that routine with a weight-training program recommended by team trainer Jack Rockwell. Sure enough, Bill showed great improvement in muscle strength and endurance. Gradually, he built his daily jogging up to five-seven miles.

"I've built back my stamina, now I've got to go for speed with sprints," he said, *"and I've got to get my timing back on hand-offs."*[9] So Bill started workouts with center DeMarco,

quarterback Johnson, and other backfield men.

While watching Cardinals' games on television, Triplett always liked the way Willis Crenshaw ran the football. Crenshaw punished oncoming tacklers, and Trip was the same style of runner.

"I've been studying game films and I've learned a lot," said Bill. *"I've seen on power sweeps how the best ball-carriers use their blockers to the best advantage. Staying behind them until just the right instant, even putting a hand on one side of the blocker's back or the other to signal which way to take the defensive player to the runner's best advantage."*[10]

Bill also watched the NFL's leading backfield aces in pass receiving, mainly to improve his ball-catching. To gain a better grip on throwing the halfback pass. When the 1965 campaign opened, Triplett was ready to play. He adjusted to the new team quickly. Little by little, he strengthened the Cards' outside running game and passing capabilities.

"I've always had an ambition to win Pro Bowl and All-League honors,"[11] said comeback-bound Triplett. *"And I think this season I ought to have a chance, because the team should be a strong contender. It would be nice, too, to include 1000-yard honors...I weigh 215 now and expect to play at that weight."*[12] He had played at 207 before his sickness.

The Cardinals, however, began the season on a sour note. They dropped their opener to Philadelphia at Franklin Field. In the loss, Conrad, Smith, and Triplett caught a total of 17 passes. They helped the Big Red offense put three touchdowns and two field goals on the scoreboard. It just wasn't enough.

<u>Browns</u>. The next week, St. Louis bounced back at Cleveland Stadium. They routed the Cleveland Browns 49-13 with a fast-paced offense and durable defense. Triplett's 4-yard burst over right tackle was the surprise of the game. Matter of fact, he left 80,161 fans in a state of shock. The play used "Thunder" Thornton as a decoy. Thornton took a fake hand-off into the left side of the line. Then Triplett blazed in from the left-halfback position to take the hand-off over right tackle.

"Thunder lined up wrong, but the play worked anyhow,"[13] said quarterback Johnson. Instead of lining up just

behind the center, Thunder took a position just a little to the right of where he was supposed to be. So it worked...so who could complain? In their goal line defense, the Browns had their middle-linebacker key on the Cards' fullback. So, when Thunder moved to the right, he set up the middle-linebacker right <u>behind</u> Triplett's running path.

"But when Thornton swung to the left, the linebacker moved over with him, and then froze when he saw his mistake," said Johnson. *"...he was out of the play when Triplett went through."*[14]

The score capped a Big Red 56-yard, seven-play surge. It increased the Cards' lead to 21-10. They put more points on the board in the second and third period. And the St. Louis defense did its part, giving the offense more opportunities to score.

"Our defense was wonderful," Coach Lemm said. *"Those interceptions, of course, give the quarterback more opportunities. On the other hand, Cleveland made their share of mistakes that blew things out of proportion."*[15]"

We didn't do much of anything right," lamented Coach Collier, *"and our mistakes were well distributed. No one player had a mortgage on them."*[16]

<u>Cowboys</u>. Nevertheless, St. Louis was in for a struggle against the Dallas Cowboys. They played on a chilly night in their home opener at Busch Stadium. The Big Red was <u>relieved</u>, even felt <u>lucky</u> to go home with a win over Dallas. The win squeaked out a four-way tie for first place in the Eastern Conference: St. Louis, Dallas, Cleveland, and New York.

Leading by only a 14-7 margin at the start of the third period, Johnson had to rely on the Cards' running game. "Comeback" Bill Triplett reminded fans of his 1963 style, rushing for 93 yards in 22 tries for a 4.2-yard average. Keeping the ball on the ground, Johnson led an attack that racked up 16 first downs and two first-half touchdowns. Triplett's versatile running worked well in that kind of offense, as he blasted into the end zone for one of those scores.

<u>Redskins</u>. Three weeks later at Busch Stadium, many fans were on hand to watch the Cardinals take their second defeat, after four straight victories.

It was Washington's first victory of the campaign under its new team president. Sam Huff presented him with the game ball after the 24-20 win over St. Louis. Triplett caught four passes for 60 yards. He scored a fourth-period touchdown from two yards out. The whole team was trying to stay in reach of possible victory. But "in reach" is not enough.

At least the week was not a total loss. St. Louis sports fans had one thing to feel good about. In pro basketball, the St. Louis Hawks, riddled by mistakes, still managed to defeat the Boston Celtics 120-110. Well, the Big Red showed as much <u>heart</u> as the Hawks. The Hawks made up for their errors on the court to produce a win. But the Cards fell short.

<u>Giants</u>. Although the Cardinals lost another close one the following week to the Giants, they put out a great team effort. And team effort is the true hallmark of champions. Triplett's triple-good performance reflected those hallmarks. The midseason game was a day for runners, and Trip put out his best effort of the season. The whole team was trying to up-end the Giants at Yankee Stadium.

In a soft voice, Luke Owens spoke about Bill's older brother, Mel—former star fullback for the Giants. From his encounters with Mel in pro-ball and college, Owens recalled a difference between Mel's and Bill's running styles.

"Mel had a stocky build and powerful legs. He was a consistent ball carrier for five-yard bursts," Luke said. *"Mel was the kind who might carry the ball 30 times in a game — but not the type, like Bill, who may go all the way when he sees daylight."*[17]

St. Louis scored only twice—a field goal and a touchdown. They were within scoring range seven other times, to no avail. Their inability to score gave the Giants extra chances to score. And score they did: two second-half touchdowns for a comeback victory.

Triplett rushed for 176 yards in 23 attempts, including a 59-yard around-end touchdown scamper. The totals went into the records as the second-best performance in Cardinals' football history. They were just a bit behind John David Crow's top day of 203 yards against the Steelers in 1960. That day, Bill also topped Mel's best-ever game for the Giants: 138 yards against the Browns in 1960.

Triplett's touchdown run came in the second period, behind pulling-guards Irv Goode and Ken Gray.

<u>Steelers</u>. The Cards restored their title hopes in the next game. They beat the Pittsburgh Steelers. With a 5-3 record, the Big Red took possession of second place in the conference. They were just ahead of New York, who had lost to Washington.

Triplett spurred the Cardinals to the win. Wilson's pass interception had given the Cards possession. Then in the second quarter, Bill crashed into the end zone for a 3-yard touchdown. The touchdown overcame a 3-0 Steelers' lead from a Mike Clark field goal. Although the Steelers played tough defense most of the time, the Cards' offense was stronger. They penetrated the "steel shell" for a 21-17 victory.

<u>Eagles</u>. Once again, however, St. Louis regressed. They dropped their third straight game, losing to the Eagles at Busch Stadium. Even then, Triplett ground out 50 yards in eight carries for a 6.2 average. That yardage kept the Big Red alive in their closely fought 28-24 defeat. But Johnson's receivers dropped some important passes.

And so, once more, the Cleveland Browns emerged as the Eastern Conference champions for the second straight year. After the Browns won over the Steelers, and with St. Louis's loss to the Eagles, they had reason to celebrate. Happy Browns in the locker room at Pitt Stadium "whooped it up" in various states of disarray.

"We're in, baby," shouted a husky young man, dashing into the showers to spread the news that the Cardinals had been eliminated."[18]

<u>Rams...downhill</u>. The St. Louis crowd probably got more thrills from the music than from the home team the next week. The Southern Illinois University marching band showed more inspiration than usual when they presented the national anthem before game time. The anthem began with a trumpet solo, and the entire band joined in by sections. Spectators in the stadium seemed more enthusiastic over the band than with the game. Just as well. At Busch Stadium, the crumpled Card offense

could not get it put together. They suffered a defeat in blue-sky weather by the Los Angeles Rams.

<u>Browns</u>. In the last game, St. Louis did manage to come back in team inspiration, but not in total points. They lost a hotly contested battle to the Browns in the season finale, 27-24. Even though the Cardinals did not fare well in total wins, some individual players stood out as real champions. Almost as if they were trying to make up for team inconsistencies.

One of those players was Bill Triplett. He made a great comeback from the lung infection that kept him out of the line-up during 1964. Mostly, during the off season, Trip began speaking of his first "comeback in life."

He became a dedicated speaker against high school drop-outs. Guest lectures became part of his off-season work in the Community Relations Department of the St. Louis Police Department. Usually, he spoke about the time he almost left high school. He changed his thinking about staying in school after he heard a prominent sports figure speak on the subject.

Students would stand up sometimes and challenge him. *"It's easy for you to preach, you're Bill Triplett."*[19]

Bill always countered with the story of his toughest time and his first "comeback." *"When I was a sophomore in high school, I was looking forward to just one thing: getting out,"* he said. *"Then I was fortunate enough to hear Rev. Bob Richards, the Olympic champion, speak at school. He associated the good student with the good champion and the good citizen...I'd had this dream about being a pro football player and, listening to him, it dawned on me that the only way I'd play pro football would be to study, and make the grade in college."*[20]

From that point on, Triplett learned his lessons well in school and on the football field. He went on to accept challenges in both college and pro-football.

When the 1965 campaign was over, Triplett had rushed for 617 yards in 174 tries, a 3.5 average, and had scored six touchdowns. He finished as the club's top ground gainer. This record gave Trip ninth place on the NFL rushing list. Bill was also effective as a pass receiver. He made 26 catches for 256 yards (9.8 average) and one touchdown.

Someone asked Triplett if he had any misgivings about a comeback. He said, "I never was discouraged. I never did believe I was finished." His comeback truly was one of the greatest ever seen in the NFL. The <u>quantity</u> of his belief-- his never giving up, never quitting--became the <u>quality</u> of courage.

How many high school students today will change their minds? Will stay in school because they heard a great athlete say the same things Triplett did? Who can convince them that, of 30 million kids taking part in U.S. sports programs every year, only a handful--maybe 200--will ever become professional players? That whatever they're dreaming of <u>depends</u> on their finishing high school?

REHABILITATION

During the winter months, Triplett persevered in his work with the police department. He went to lots and lots of inner-city schools to show films. To talk to students about personal safety. Triplett usually showed a film from the Ohio State Highway Patrol titled, "At The Scene Of Accidents," and Bill said it was "a real shocker." He emphasized, *"It's more effective than an animated cartoon, isn't it?"*[1]

Trip explained--after showing the film at St. Anthony's High School one day--that a proficient safety program was possible for each individual. He spoke directly and especially to girls in the group.

"If a young man takes you on a date and is a showoff and careless driver or both, tell him to take you home. Then spread the word around that he's a bad driver and you won't go out with him. I guess you've heard that young men are interested in dating young ladies."[2]

He also expressed a <u>serious</u> attitude about the significance of safety. Audiences responded seriously, too.

"I don't know about St. Louis driving," Triplett said later to the department manager, Bill Handy. *"My wife and I have decided to make St. Louis our permanent home, and we'll live here even if I'm traded--which is something you always have to consider in pro sports. But I don't think I'll ever learn to live like a native, with the drivers rolling through stop signs. The first half-hour I spent in St. Louis, riding from the airport to the hotel, I saw a man go through a stop sign and hit another car, back up, and drive off. I thought, oh-oh, what goes on in this city? And I'm still wondering, at stop signs."*[3]

Bill became a celebrity speaker in St. Louis. He received increasingly lucrative offers to work off-season with groups other than the police department. That was unfortunate, because Triplett was interested in giving his time to public service. He wanted to repay society for his early successes. And he was genuinely grateful for his work in the Cardinals' public relations unit.

One time someone asked about the general attitude of juveniles in the city. Triplett answered by speaking of the problem of street interrogations.

"It works two ways," he said. *"I've seen officers get abuse from kids no man should be asked to take. But other kids. who have never been in any kind of trouble. have the right to expect courtesy if they are questioned."*[4]

"There were so many kids." Bill continued, *"good students and leaders in their classes. who complained about harassment that you had to believe some of them were right. I'm really in no position to give advice."* he said, *"except that some officers might get more cooperation by being polite to* <u>all</u> *kids in the beginning. even though they leave themselves open for a smart aleck answer, or no answer at all. It's hard to figure."* he added. *"When I was a kid. we shook in our shoes in front of a policeman. even though he was pleasant and we were doing nothing wrong. We knew he represented authority."*[5]

Whether he was riding along on cruiser duty or walking a foot patrol. Triplett recognized a survival instinct among both policemen and criminals. *"An officer in plain clothes and an unmarked car could say, 'Those guys are up to no good...' and as soon as they saw the car. the guys he pointed out would take off."*

As a professional athlete. Bill went all out, "full tilt," every season just as if <u>everything</u> was on the line. One reason was that he always faced stiff competition at the first-string halfback-fullback spot. He brought excellent characteristics, however, to the Cards' training camp: his quiet determination and <u>guts</u>.

Each year, Triplett received the best wishes of everyone in the police department for the next season. And all those wishes were sincere. On the whole, though, Trip was more inclined to live in a small town instead of a big city. He expressed his feelings one time, when he told of being recruited by a major college.

"They took me to the Rose Bowl as their guest." he said. *"and it was too much. just too big for a boy from a small town. I decided to go to a school more my size and style. I went to Miami."*[6]

Although Bill was happy in his dual-career. he was about to

face his second disappointment. The 1966 campaign began, and St. Louis coaches were making changes. New head coach Charlie Winner was a rah-rah, gung-ho individual. He took Trip out of the line-up as the Cardinals' first-string left-halfback. Of course, lots of friends and fans saw this shift as an injustice to a great player. Trip had led the Big Red ground attack the previous year -- ahead of Joe Childress, Prentice Gautt, Willie Crenshaw, and "Thunder" Thornton. Before the 1965 season, the Cardinals had even traded John David Crow just to factor Trip into their long-range plans.

But Bill ran the ball only 13 times during the 1966 season. He did not play at all from midseason on. And the Cards dropped from first to fourth place in the Eastern Conference. While being interviewed, good natured, soft spoken Triplett explained what was happening. *"They had this young fellow named Johnny Roland, and they had paid him a lot of money to play halfback."* Everybody knew there was more to it than that. And Triplett will admit there was a personality conflict between him and Charlie Winner.

"I'm not one of these fellows who shows a lot of emotion," said Triplett. *"I can't be rah-rah. I build a fire within myself, and when it's ready to come out, I am ready to play. That's the way I am, and that's the way I've been all my career, going back to high school."*[7]

<u>Detour to New York</u>.

Trip did not "fulfill the expectations" of the Big Red coaching staff. So they traded him to the Giants that year. The trade did <u>not</u> catch him off guard.

"I've been preparing myself mentally for a change the last year and a half," he said realistically. *"I mean, when you're sitting there and you know you've led the team in running, and you're 100 per cent, and they don't even use you a few plays to spell the running back, something's wrong. I knew I had to go."*[8]

The New York Giants, of course, were Triplett's dream team. He'd wanted to play for the Giants when he was still in high school. It was only natural: he wanted to follow in his brother Mel's footsteps as a New Yorker backfield man. In training camp at Fairfield University, before the 1967 season, coach Allie Sherman promised Bill a definite chance at the first-string halfback slot.

If Bill won the starting position, he also wanted to accomplish some personal goals. Like, he wanted to break Mel's club records: most rushing touchdowns in a single game (3) and most points in a game (18). But Trip played only sparingly for the Giants. He got his hands on the ball only 72 times, racking up 379 all-purpose yards for the season. On to Detroit.

So, Triplett's career with New York was short-lived. The Giants traded him and Bill Swain to the Detroit Lions that winter in exchange for Bruce Maher. Trip endured his setbacks as a pro football player. And he got back to true form in the Lions' starting line-up. But he didn't ever quite reach that pinnacle of success he'd reached as a leading ground-gainer with St. Louis.

Cowboys. The Cowboys crushed the Lions in the 1968 campaign opener at the Cotton Bowl, 59-13.

Even though they were in for a dismal season, Detroit fielded a great team. They had a nucleus of outstanding players who had to be reckoned with each and every week.

Packers. That old adage about "defense winning games" was even more true when the Lions played Green Bay. In that game the Lions battled the Packers to a 14-14 tie. The Phil Bengston-coached Packers were out to avenge their 23-17 loss to Detroit three weeks before--at Green Bay.

Triplett banged out seven yards, then two more in the first quarter. Those runs helped Detroit make a first down at the Packer 40-yard line. On the next play, Munson led McCullouch on a perfect pass-strike for a touchdown. Trip's running supported the Lions' passing game later in the period, too. Munson connected with McCullouch neatly for another touchdown and a 14-0 lead. Only 6:28 minutes had expired in the first quarter!

In the third period, the Packers came back on a Bratkowski pass to Carroll Dale. Touchdown! In the final quarter, Bart Starr entered the game. Quickly, he threw a touchdown strike to Boyd Dowler, tying the game and ending the scoring.

Rams. Even though Detroit was struggling for victories, Triplett kept himself mentally ready to play. At 6'2" and 212 pounds, he used the power and speed of his running style to battle the Los Angeles Rams in game #8. The Rams edged the Lions on a 31-yard field goal by Gossett, just before intermission. No scoring took place in the second half, and the Rams held onto a 10-7 victory.

<u>Colts</u>. The next week at Detroit's Tiger Stadium, Trip led the Lions in rushing yardage once more. Detroit fans went away disappointed when the Colts came out on top at the last whistle. Even in defeat, however, Triplett set an example of mental toughness on the field. He always pursued victory intensely, especially when the going got tough in a come-from-behind situation.

<u>Falcons</u>. Sure enough, the Lions showed great resilience when they beat the Atlanta Falcons. Nobody "gave up" because of earlier frustrations, and Detroit made a classic comeback. They chalked up an inspiring triumph, lifting team spirits. Atlanta bounced back when "Cannonball" Butler broke loose to his right side. He made a 60-yard touchdown gallop for Atlanta's only score.

<u>Redskins</u>. The Joe Schmidt-coached Detroit Lions fell short of winning the season finale at Washington. Otto Graham's Redskins put on a non-stoppable offensive drive in the fourth period. They dominated the Lions with a 14-3 win before 50,123 fans.

Although Detroit didn't win all the time in 1968, at least they had the satisfaction of knowing they tried.

As President Theodore Roosevelt said: "It is not the critic that counts...the credit belongs to the man who is actually in the arena...who strives valiantly, who errs and often comes up short again and again...who, at the best, knows in the end the triumph of high achievement, and who at worse, if he fails, at least fails while daring greatly, so that his place shall never be with those cold and timid souls who know neither victory nor defeat.[9]

Even in defeat, certain Lions kept the spirit, the will to win, and met both team and personal challenges each week.

Bill Triplett in another "comeback" was the club's second-leading ground gainer.

Another season.

In 1969, the Detroit Lions ranked first in quality of player talent in the NFL's Central Division, Western Conference. Football experts expected them to win the conference championship.

Their passing game centered around superb athletes such as quarterback Bill Munson. He was the NFL's #7 passer the previous year. Receivers Earl McCullouch and tight-end Charlie Sanders were back, too. Also, a top-quality backfield featured Bill Triplett, Mel Farr, Nick Eddy, and rookie Altie Taylor. Triplett was a key figure at fullback in the Lions' backfield. He would become the club's leading rusher -- picking up the load.

Steelers. The Lions entered their 1969 regular season with a series of five straight pre-season victories and one defeat. But at Pittsburgh, the Steelers upset the Lions by a close margin, 16-13. The Lions made some costly mistakes, and the Steelers were a determined ball club. They took advantage of every Lion glitch.

Detroit took a 3-0 lead early in the game. Mann kicked a 23-yard field goal after they recovered a Steeler fumble on the 29-yard line. What was disappointing: just before the field goal, Munson watched Triplett drop a sure touchdown pass.

In the fourth quarter, Alex Karras recovered a Pittsburgh fumble on the Steeler 27-yard line, and Detroit moved ahead again. Pittsburgh on their next possession, however, marched straight down the field. They took the lead after the kickoff, and Brankston made the last score of the game.

Giants. Although their loss to the Steelers was a disappointment, the Lions were determined. They came back the next week to shut out the Giants, 24-0. By midseason, Detroit had a heavy-duty passing attack that dove-tailed with an explosive running game.

Falcons. After their win over San Francisco, the Lions returned home the following week, Triplett had another good day rushing. He gave the Lions an offensive surge on their scoring drives. Trip himself scored a touchdown from the 1-yard line, giving the Lions a second-quarter 14-0 lead over Atlanta. Detroit managed to score only three second-half points. But they were able to hold off an Atlanta rally in the final minutes of the game and win 27-21.

Packers. Two weeks later, Detroit went to Green Bay to play before a fanatic Packer crowd at Lambeau Field. The Lions marched 65 yards on their opening drive. On a fake punt, on his usual blocking route for Lem Barney, Triplett took the snap pass from center and waltzed around right end to the Green Bay 16. It showed Detroit's offensive might as they went on to victory.

Colts. Some fans were ready for action two weeks later in Baltimore. Detroit was about to take on the Colts in a rain-soaked, snow-covered Memorial Stadium. The Colts scored first on Michaels' 12-yard field goal. But the Lions retaliated. Munson directed Detroit to the Colts' 23-yard line. From there, Triplett broke loose through the middle of the line and went the distance for the touchdown. A little later, the Lions scored again. And so did Baltimore as the game ended in a 17-17 tie.

Rams. In their next game, the Lions hit pay dirt first, taking an early first-quarter lead. They used only eight plays to cover the distance. The Rams didn't even cross midfield until late in the period. Then Lem Barney recovered a Los Angeles fumble at the 10 and returned it to the 25-yard line. A little later, Munson threw an aerial bomb to Triplett at the Ram's 24. Bill was all alone as he raced into the end zone, completing a 62-yard touchdown play.

A strong Detroit defense thwarted the Rams in the third period, and the visitors had to punt. The Lions took over on their own 38 and marched right on down to the Los Angeles 15-yard line. Triplett's and Altie Taylor's outstanding running set up Mann's 22-yard boot over the crossbar. Suddenly, Detroit had a 22-0 lead. Mann booted two more field goals in the fourth period, and the Lions aced a 28-0 shut-out win. Triplett at the end of the game, was the team's "top gun."

Bears. The Detroit vs. Chicago Bears finale was played at Wrigley Field. They watched in dismay while LeBeau intercepted a Concannon pass early in the game. Four plays later, the Lions scored. After a series of late third-period punt exchanges, Weger intercepted another Concannon aerial and returned it to the two--with less than four minutes remaining. Triplett took the hand-off and hammered over tackle for the touchdown. Mann converted. The Lions won, 20-3.

About star status: Triplett finished the campaign as the Lions' top ground-gainer. With his longest touchdown run of 62 yards against the L. A. Rams. So Triplett carried the load for the backfield. He led the Detroit Lions (9-4-1) to second place in the NFL's Central Division of the Western Conference--behind their first-place nemesis, the Minnesota Vikings.

New day, new dollar.

As the 1970 campaign began, some football experts noted that Triplett gained only 377 yards rushing in 1969. On a good day, those scores would have been all in a day's work for Gale Sayers, Calvin Hill, or Tom Matte. Yet Trip's record surpassed the performances of his teammates, who had got most of the pre-season publicity.

The reason for Trip doing so well was his durability, mental readiness, and desire to excel. He just never got the big build-up. He was not a No. 1 draft pick. All he did was get the job done. Nick Eddy, Notre Dame All-American, had received $250,000 a few years before. With illness and injuries, he had played sparingly during the previous two seasons, accumulating only 448 yards rushing.

Mel Farr received a lot less than Eddy, but he played more and played better. Mel ground out 245 yards in the first four games the previous year. Later, he was sidelined with an injury. As a rookie, Altie Taylor lacked experience. He didn't perform as a top notch player in 1969. So... comparisons, comparisons.

When the 1970 season finally got under way, Mel Farr and Nick Eddy were physically rehabilitated. Altie Taylor had enough playing experience to make him a much better, smarter runner. Also, the Lions had signed Oklahoma's Heisman Trophy winner, Steve Owens.

Where did this leave Triplett? It left him as the fifth backfield man with a starting position on the kickoff return team. So Trip carried the ball only 48 times for 156 yards and one touchdown during the entire season. He played on the kickoff return team for the 10-4-0 Lions. Period. Still, at the start of the 1971 season, Coach Schmidt named Triplett special teams captain. Trip remained in this role until the end of his career, after the 1972 season.

Coach Schmidt spoke of the importance of having a special teams captain and his selection of Triplett for the job. He was answering questions at an after-practice press conference. *"We think it's an important part of the game. and it's important to have someone in there to make decisions when they're on the field,"* Schmidt said. *"Triplett is well suited for that. and he's been doing a good job for us on our special teams."*[10]

The Lions, unlike other NFL teams, seldom had had a special teams captain. On occasion, regular team captain John Gordy. Alex Karras, or Ron Goovert did the decision making. *"It's not just an honor. There's responsibility,"* said Triplett. A 31-year-old veteran, Triplett was in his fourth season as a Lion. *"I have to make the calls on punt and kickoff teams...whether they're overloading the blocking or not, things like that."*[11]

Bill was on all the special teams except the punt return team. He made sure everybody on the teams was alert and hustling. The outstanding special teams player of the week was awarded the game ball--a choice voted on by all three team captains. When appointing Triplett. Schmidt made it clear about the importance of special teams in the NFL.

"People who watch realize how important special teams are on returns and coverage," he said. *"We figure to win three or four. sometimes five games a year on the special teams--we have in the past...This includes the field goal teams. kickoff, and punt returns and so forth. They came up with the big plays like blocking field goals or punts, forcing and recovering fumbles. long returns. etc."*[12]

Thus, along with his jobs as part-time runner and strong blocker, Triplett took on new responsibilities. They called him "Captain Bill And His Bomb Squad."

Bill Triplett - Courtesy of Detroit Football Lions

DE-FENSE !

For many years, Youngstown Sheet and Tube Company was the economic hub of its community, but the company died in 1976. Sheet and Tube had built a tradition of producing the best bar and pipe steel anywhere. Not only in the steel valley region, but the entire United States.

Before the company closed its doors, however, it had become one of many American dinosaurs in the steel industry's "rust belt." That "belt" includes most of the Great Lakes region. Like the automobile industry, domestic oil, and the semiconductor industry, the steel industry took second place in the world market. Sheet and Tube closed its doors--a victim of forces bigger than the towns, the state, or the nation.

During its years of prosperity, various ethnic groups made up Sheet and Tube's work force. First and second generation Poles, Slovaks, Italians, Greeks...you name them: they were there. They believed in the American work ethic, the American Dream. Believed it gave them a quality of life not available anywhere else in the world. As a big part of that life, almost everyone took in Friday night high school football at Memorial John Knapick Stadium. They liked to watch Campbell Memorial teams in Steel Valley Conference play.

Football tradition at Campbell grew along with steel production in the whole steel valley region. Tradition has survived to this day, long after Sheet and Tube has gone. The 1989 Campbell Memorial squad finished as state runners-up in Division III, and its 1990 team was regional champion. Memorial ranked #1 in Ohio's football polls the entire year.

Because of changes in team competition, only five teams belong to the SVC today: Austintown Fitch, Youngstown Boardman, Youngstown Cardinal Mooney, Warren G. Harding, and Youngstown Ursuline. Of the original 1949 charter teams, only two remain: Austintown Fitch and Boardman. Still, the SVC ranks as one of Ohio's great high school football conferences.

<u>Ad astra</u>...

Bob Babich grew up in the rugged steel mill town of Campbell, Ohio. He was a star linebacker for Campbell Memorial in the middle 1960's. His record is one of the cornerstones of the SVC's long football tradition.

Bob grew up interested in football because his father liked it so well. Because of community influences, too. Bob's father worked for the Sheet and Tube. He did <u>not</u> want his son to work there after finishing high school, however. Both Bob's parents insisted on his getting an education along with playing football.

When Bob was in high school, he had already made going to college his number one goal. He never lost sight of that goal, either, especially after playing football for two great coaches: Johnny Knapick and Sloko Gill. Babich played his sophomore and junior years for head coach Knapick. Knapick was a long time teacher-coach (42 years) at Campbell Memorial. Coach Knapick directed Campbell Memorial to six Steel Valley Conference championships during his tenure at the school.

Knapick was a traditional coach, nearly everyone's <u>ideal</u> coach. He taught good sportsmanship, discipline, a 100% effort on the field, classroom work, and <u>life after football</u>. He also taught high school English: a fairly rare combination with football. Of course, if need be, Knapick could give a player a kick-in-the-pants to increase his motivation. Babich respected all that.

Bob played his senior year under head coach Sloko Gill. Gill guided the Red Devils to their final SVC championship that year, 1964. A standout football player at Youngstown College and professional player with the Detroit Lions, Gill brought excellent coaching skills to the Campbell team and to the conference.

As a linebacker for the Campbell Red Devils, Babich was an All-SVC first-team selection in both his junior and senior years. He was first-team All-Ohio his senior season and played in Ohio's North-South All-Star game that summer. As a high school senior, Bob's greatest honor was recognition of his role in Campbell Memorial's SVC Championship, symbolized by the Ingot Award Trophy.

After football season, Babich stayed in good physical condition, working out and playing baseball for his school. He achieved success during his senior year, pitching a three-hitter in the Boardman game, helping the Red Devils warm up for regional play.

Today, Babich believes that growing up in Campbell's rich mix of ethnic groups prepared him to get along with a lot of different types of people. Babich is of Slovak-Hungarian descent. He believes that his own ancestry made it easier for him to get along socially, both in college and in professional football.

After Babich's senior year, he received offers of football scholarships from a lot of colleges and universities. The list included Ohio State. *"Woody Hayes was after me fairly hard,"* said Bob. Other Big Ten schools, too, plus Syracuse, Penn State, and Miami (Ohio) University. Bob chose Miami (Ohio) University, called the "Cradle of Coaches," rather than the bigger schools' offers. He was happy about his decision and pleased with the way head coach Bo Schembechler recruited him.

"I was looking for a school where I could play two or three years of varsity football," Babich remembered. *"I want to be a coach some day, and Miami is the place to learn that, and—I meant it—I liked Bo Schembechler's style."*[1] Babich found Miami all he'd hoped for. He was the Redskins middle linebacker (1966-68) under coach Schembechler.

Babich was the youngest player ever to be inducted into Miami's Athletic Hall of Fame. Also, he was a first team All-American linebacker selection in 1968. His teammates twice voted him "Most Valuable Player." He was Miami's "Athlete of the Year" during the 1968 '69 academic year. A two-time All-Mid American Conference linebacker, unanimously selected. "Defensive Player of the Year" in the MAC (1968) and his team's captain that same year.

There's more...! Bob was also selected first team All-American by <u>Playboy</u> magazine's pre-season pick, <u>Time</u> magazine, Kodak's All-American coaches' selections, Football Coaches Association, and the <u>Sporting News</u>. He played in the American, North-South, and Senior Bowls. Also, he played a great game in the College All-Star Game in Chicago against the defending

Super Bowl Champion New York Jets. His performances on the field insured that he would be a first-round draft pick by the San Diego Chargers in the spring of 1969.

In Bob's junior season as the Redskins' middle linebacker, he accumulated 109 solo tackles and 55 assisted. He made 99 solo tackles and 55 assisted as a senior. One's mind boggles. Think of all this now: Babich became the first first-team Consensus All-American ever to be picked from Miami (Ohio) University and the first from the Mid-American Conference.

Coach "Bo" Schembechler figured Babich would be an All-American middle-linebacker. *"Babich is the best defensive footballer I ever coached,"* Schembechler said emphatically. Bo's comments came at a press conference late in August, just before the start of the Redskins' 1968 season. Quite a statement by such a coach. Schembechler was an assistant at Northwestern and Ohio State before taking the head job at Miami. And Miami has "hatched" so many great coaches: Earl Blaik, Paul Brown, Paul Dietzel, Weeb Ewbank, Warren Ott, Ara Parseghian, Bo Schembechler, and Woody Hayes.

Babich was always committed to excellence. It showed in his tenacity on the field. He also simply loved the game, enjoyed body-contact sports.

"I love contact on the football field. I like to hit people. I'm anxious to have a fine season and get a chance with the pro football world," he said. *"I like defense. I think there's something electrifying about hitting someone with the ball."*[2]

"Pro scouts have been flocking around like flies to watch Babich," commented Schembechler. *"Figure for his size, a 4.7 mark for the 40-yard dash and you know he can move like a back. He's terrific. Scouts say he's the finest middle- linebacker they've seen in years."*[3]

Babich was durable and consistent. At 6'1" and 225 pounds, he didn't miss a minute of defense during his last two seasons-- and with no injuries. Coach Schembechler praised Bob for his best defensive game against Indiana the previous year. But then "Bo" added, *"He never had a bad game. He's a coach's dream on defense."*[4]

Babich, however, rates his performance in the 14-3 victory

over Tulane as his best. Bob was all-everything in that game. He also made lineman of the week in the following week. Bob showed how great he was in the 1969 Miami-Kent State game. The Miami defense held Kent quarterback Steve Trustdorf--the nation's sixth leading passer--to only 42 yards passing.

Babich led the defense on just about every play. Late in the fourth period, Trustdorf marched Kent State to the Miami 10-yard line. But on third and five, Babich blitzed Kent's offense and threw Trustdorf for a 13-yard loss. Babich rushed through on the next play, throwing Trustdorf for a 10-yard loss. Then he recovered a Kent State fumble. He couldn't lose for winning! Of course, Miami defeated Kent State that day.

"I'm not a professional football coach, but if they want speed, a hard-nosed player, then Babich is it."[5] Bo said.

That's just what the San Diego Chargers had in mind when they drafted Babich. The football world was real high on Bob. Time magazine did a special feature on him and 21 other top college prospects. One professional scout called Babich "the best linebacker in collegiate football."

At the beginning of the 1969 season, Babich was doing what all the experts predicted, playing his best at middle- linebacker for the Chargers. Then Bob met with a stroke of really bad luck. In a preseason game with the Cleveland Browns, Babich sustained a bad knee injury. Tore the tendons. That injury kept him out of football the entire season. He lost out on rookie-of-the-year honors. The San Diego fans felt bad, because Babich had come in as an instant success. He was making tackles all over the field before the injury.

Chargers' head coach Sid Gillman felt terrible about Bob's injury. San Diego had lost their best linebacker prospect for the entire campaign.

Mrs. Babich, Bob's mother, felt worse than anybody. She boarded a plane for San Diego as soon as she could to be with her injured son. She always referred to him as "Bobby." As his mother, knowing that football was Bobby's whole life, she was enormously concerned. The Chargers made arrangements for Mrs. Babich's stay in California.

Of course, Bob told his mother not to worry. He knew he

would come back and play again. Play would not be possible until the 1970 season, however, according to medical reports. They operated on the knee right away. Surgeons had a high percentage of success with Bob's type of injury, and Sid Gillman made sure Bob got the best treatment.

Mrs. Babich had seen the injury happen on television at a neighbor's house. They were watching a Cleveland station through a special broadcast frequency. She recalled Bobby's doing a fine job on the first two tackles of the game. Then it happened on the third scrimmage play. A terrible feeling!

"Yes, I said, 'I know.' It was a stupid thing to say. 'I know.' How the hell did I know?" Mrs. Babich smiled. *"I kept saying, get up, get up.....You see him lying there, and you have no idea what it is. All you want is to see him get up. The next time I saw him, they showed a shot of him pointing out to the field. The doctor told me later, on the phone. he said he wasn't going to any hospital. He was going back into the game.'*[6]

With Bob's determination, of course, it was certain he would play again. Bob never got discouraged during the following months of rehabilitation with weights and leg exercises. Bob's mom knew he would not give up. Neither of his parents worried about him. They'd had only one rule at home: No matrimony! *"If you want a good education. you can't think about marriage,"*[7] said Mrs. Babich.

Bob's parents were hoping that he would go to school and get his master's degree instead of "doing nothing" for a year. Mrs. Babich commented, *"You need that good education. You can't tell, I'm sure he'll play again, but..."*[8]

Bob's mother was still proud of the fact that Bobby was San Diego's #1 choice. He and quarterback Marty Domres were chosen together as first choices. Bob, too, was extremely happy about it. He hadn't thought he would be picked so soon because Miami was such a small college. Bob and Marty were friends, rooting for each other to make it!

While he was in high school and college, Babich never sustained an injury. The family kept scrapbooks for each year. Of course, Mrs. Babich put them together. She had just started a new one with the coach's game in Atlanta and the All-Star game in Chicago. Bob was thrilled about a picture his mom had of his sacking quarterback Joe Namath in the Chicago game. It turned up in <u>Sports illustrated</u>.

As the plane got closer to Los Angeles International Airport, Mrs. Babich talked with Al Barlick and Ed Vargo, the umpires. She told them she would be rooting for Marty Domres to beat out John Hadl at quarterback. She spoke <u>adamantly</u> about Marty's success at becoming first string. They talked about her son and Youngstown and, after getting off the plane, they said they would be pulling for Bob to come back.

"He will," she said. *"I brought my radio along. We'll listen to your ball game tonight."*[9] And she walked off into the airport.

Mrs. Babich understood her son very well--his desire, determination, and dedication to the sport. And so did Mike Maylen, the Chargers' special-training activities coach. Mike arranged a weightlifting program for Bob--to rehabilitate his injured knee and to bring him back 100% physically. *"I'll be ready when practice starts in July,"*[10] insisted Babich.

Maylen believed Babich was the strongest linebacker in pro football! *"When it comes to weightlifting, he has done 245 pounds in a sitting press. Weightlifting-wise, that's why I say he's the strongest. That's fantastic."*[11]

It was a rigorous program and Babich worked at it six days a week. Three days a week--Monday, Wednesday and Friday--Babich developed the bicep and tricep muscles. Three days a week--Tuesday, Thursday and Saturday--he concentrated on programmed stress development of the leg and chest area. He ran 45 minutes everyday on a special jogging machine. *"Dedication, that's the key for Babich and he'll be a great success,"* said Maylen. *"When the Chargers signed Babich, I arranged a program for him while [he was still] in school. He boosted his weight from 214 to 232 pounds."*[12]

Babich's determination paid off. He was ready like he said he would be when the 1970 San Diego Chargers training camp began. And by the first game, Babich had earned his place as San Diego's middle-linebacker. He still had the strength to ward off those big blocking linemen. Still had the quickness and agility to get to the ball carrier, the focal point on the run. And he still could drop back on pass coverage as an integral part of San Diego's pass protection.

<u>New conference</u>
The Baltimore Colts were San Diego's new opponent that fall in a new conference: the American Football Conference in the restructured NFL. Big John Unitas was 37 years of age and still respected as a great quarterback, regardless of the new conference debut. And the old pro depended on himself to direct the Colts' offense. He led a final drive that set up Jim O'Brian's game-winning field goal. That field goal gave the Colts a 16-14 triumph in the final 56 seconds of the game.

Baltimore won a squeaker, true. But the tenacious, aroused Charger defense, led by an intense Babich, kept the Colts' scoring to three field goals and only one touchdown.

<u>Bears</u>. In this game, the Chargers captured a victory. They defeated the Chicago Bears by 20-7 before a bunch of screaming Chicago fans. Quarterback John Hadl connected on two third-period touchdown passes--one for 14 and one for 33 yards. Wide-receiver Gary Garrison caught them both for the team's victory surge.

Built around four excellent linebackers, San Diego's defense did bend a little, but it did not break. Babich, leading team tackler, headed the charge that stopped Chicago's offense.

<u>Browns</u>. During the game, San Diego capitalized on two Cleveland mistakes. Those mistakes led to two San Diego touchdowns in the second quarter. Chuck Detwiler, a defensive back, raced 25 yards on a Browns' fumble-turnover, caused by Babich, for one of the touchdowns. San Diego scored the other one after Jeff Staggs recovered a Cleveland fumble. The Chargers' defense then stopped a Browns' offensive advance. They intercepted a pass and took control of the game in the second half, and went on to win, 27-10.

<u>Patriots</u>. In game #9, 30,598 spectators crowded Boston's stadium to see San Diego play the Patriots. They watched while the Chargers moved in front and held a 16-14 lead. They were <u>not</u> delighted to see San Diego's stout defense performing well. Babich at middle-linebacker was the focal point of the defense

against Patriot runs. He was a key part of the defense against the pass, too.

"Today, the heroes of defense are those middle linebackers, and they have lent a great deal of glamour to pro football."[13]

That description went far beyond the days of sports writers who didn't even know the names of the defensive players. Actually, most of the credit for the prominence of the middle-linebacker goes to Paul Brown. Not only was Brown a great coach, but he also was a great innovator in the game. He taught his offensive guards to shift just about a foot away from the center--and the tackles to shift about 1-1/2 to 2 feet away from the guards. Their stance widened the gap between the defensive tackle and middle guard over center. This spread-out formation occurred for the first time during the 1950 campaign. Coach Brown devised it to open up Cleveland's running game against the Philadelphia Eagles' 50 defense. It changed defensive line-ups throughout the NFL. The middle guard became a middle-linebacker. And the 4-3 defense was created!

So, the San Diego defense continued to battle against its foes during the last part of the campaign. And the linebacker corps helped San Diego avenge an earlier drubbing they'd received from Kansas City. In the season finale, the score was Chargers 31, Chiefs 13. The victory gave San Diego a third-place finish in the AFC Western Division <u>behind</u> the Oakland Raiders and Kansas City Chiefs. It was San Diego's fifth consecutive third-place finish.

Over in Oakland, the San Francisco 49ers defeated the Raiders in a 38-7 triumph. Thus the 49ers finished <u>first</u> in the NFC Western Division. When George Allen's Los Angeles Rams defeated New York that same week, they inspired John Brodie to lead the 49ers to their first championship in 25 years.

<u>Total the scores.</u>

A great team player and leader, Babich finished the campaign with 173 tackles for an amazing average of 12 tackles per game. That achievement ranked him as San Diego's top tackler and one of the greatest in the AFC. After sitting out the entire

1969 season, he made an incredible comeback. Not just a "comeback"--but ranks among the great linebackers of all time.

He was totally devoted to football, determined to return to the game. By meeting the challenge of a serious physical injury, he passed an intense, personal test of courage. Lesser men would have given up. The fact that he <u>did not quit</u> places Babich among the great period leaders of our time. His record sends powerful signals to rookies today: "Hang in there...don't quit!"

OUTSIDE SHIFT

Football season could not come too soon for Babich. He was looking forward to playing a key role at middle-linebacker for the Chargers during 1971. Babich not only had enormous strength (bench pressing 475 lbs.), but he had those spartan qualities of discipline, perseverance, and determination. Above all he loved being a <u>contact</u> football player. These qualities featured in San Diego's opening victory over the Kansas City Chiefs and endured throughout the 1971 season.

<u>Kansas City</u>. A record crowd packed San Diego Jack Murphy Stadium to watch their home team turn back the rugged K.C. Chiefs. Mike Garrett raced for a 26-yard fourth-period touchdown, topping off the Chargers' offense in their 21-14 win.

Better yet, the Babich-led San Diego defense shut out Kansas City's offense in the last half. It kept the Chiefs scoreless while racking up prosperity for the Chargers.

<u>Pittsburgh</u>. The Chargers, however, had a tough time against a determined Steelers club. They played like demons after their loss to John Madden's Oakland Raiders the previous week. But Terry Bradshaw ran for a final-quarter touchdown. The Steelers defense stalled the Chargers three times inside the six-yard line. And Pittsburgh waltzed off with a 21-17 win. It was a cliff-hanger and a big disappointment.

With less than four minutes to go, San Diego came back. John Hadl moved his club to the Pittsburgh 4-yard line, but Jack Ham intercepted Hadl's pass on the next play. Oh, no! Only 1:49 minutes left. The Steelers could win by just running out the clock. But San Diego's defense hit Bradshaw hard and he fumbled. As he tried to scramble around end, Bob Babich appeared in the maze of tacklers. Babich recovered the ball at the Steelers' 20-yard line--only 1:06 minutes left. San Diego had a last-minute scoring chance and a possible victory.

Hadl moved the Chargers on a nice drive to the Pittsburgh 1-yard line, but the Chargers couldn't score. The Steeler defense stiffened, and time ran out.

<u>Defense...defense!</u>

<u>Buffalo</u>. While the offense gets the fame and the cheers from its fans, the defense wins games or championships for the team.

The success of San Diego's defense depended heavily on how well the two inside down-linemen and middle-backer (called the "middle triangle") fine-tuned their tactics. With effective effort, the defensive tackles could break up or absorb Buffalo's line blocking (or offensive interference). If they didn't make their tackles at exactly the right times, the ball carrier would be free. At the middle-linebacker spot, Babich would be responsible for picking up the tackle. And, in most cases, he would pick up the glory that makes a star out of the Sunday afternoon middleman.

<u>New York</u>. In that game, some San Diego fans could not believe San Diego's smashing triumph over the former Super Bowl Champion New York Jets. John Hadl threw for four touchdowns and rushed for one more, sparking the Chargers to a 49-21 win. The Chargers' linebackers staved off New York's second-half onslaught and advanced San Diego to victory. With 4.7 speed, Babich was smack in the middle of it all.

<u>St. Louis</u>. San Diego boosted their record one more notch two weeks later at San Diego Stadium. The Chargers' defense held St. Louis scoreless in the second half—until the final 17 seconds of the game. Then Cid Edwards bumped over from the 1-yard line giving the Cards a 17-17 tie.

Babich played well, as did his counterpart, Jamie Rivers, an outstanding middle linebacker for St. Louis. (For the record: Rivers was from Youngstown, Ohio, near Bob's hometown of Campbell. Rivers was an All-City fullback-linebacker at Youngstown South High, and he starred at Bowling Green State (Ohio) before the Cardinals drafted him. Jamie was up for rookie of the year in 1968, but he lost out because of a midseason injury.

After the tie, the Cards tried an on-side kick, but the Chargers recovered it on their own 47-yard line. The Chargers slithered by St. Louis 20-17 on Dennis Partee's 45-yard field goal just as the gun sounded.

<u>Oakland</u>. Unfortunately in the tenth game of the season, San Diego blew a 14-point halftime lead and lost by one point to the Oakland Raiders. John Madden's Raiders rallied behind

quarterback Daryle Lamonica. They pulled off the 34-33 come-from-behind squeaker in Oakland.

Babich, however, remained astonishing in the American Football Conference as one of the conference's top tacklers. Ultimately, one of the NFL's greatest. If fans wanted to know where the action was during a Chargers' game? They just looked for No. 60 on the field: middle-linebacker Bob Babich. Through the first 10 games of the campaign, Babich made 133 tackles (68 unassisted) for a game average of 13.3. That is a <u>whole lot</u> of tackles.

"What makes Bob stand out is his range." said Defensive Coach Phil Bengston. *"He is extremely mobile, has all the physical qualities, and is a fine student of the game."*[1]

At 6'1", 232-pounds, Babich believed he had improved with experience. And with the coaching of Phil Bengston. *"I'm reading better,"* said Babich. *"Situations are more clear. I know what to expect on 3rd and 5. I know more about the teams we play. Coach Bengston never mentions Green Bay, but we are playing the same type of aggressive defense he used with the Packers. I like it, and he has taught me a lot."*[2]

<u>Cincinnati</u>. Under interim Coach Harland Svare, San Diego faced the Cincinnati Bengals the next week at Riverfront Stadium. Babich and the Chargers' defense would need an outstanding game to offset Cincinnati's powerful offense. As things turned out, Hadl threw four pass-interceptions, and Cincinnati surged ahead to a 31-0 shut-out. It was the first shut-out in the Bengals four-year history. Babich dedicated himself to the game and made his usual share of tackles, but it just was not San Diego's day. Everything went right for Cincinnati.

<u>Vikings</u>. The following week at San Diego Stadium. 54.505 fans watched the Chargers try to knock Minnesota out of a sure chance at the NFC's Central Division title. The San Diego <u>defense</u> actually deserved credit for the win, because the aggressive, Babich-led tacklers held the Vikings scoreless in the second half. The Chargers thoroughly enjoyed their revenge after Minnesota's 34-7 pre-season drubbing. It was a sweet triumph for Coach Svare, too, because his team had done so poorly the previous week against Cincinnati.

"I have no idea what caused us to play so badly last week and so well today," Svare said. *"I don't even think Amos Alonzo Stagg would know. This is a crazy game."*[3]

<u>Home again</u>...

<u>Denver</u>. So, it was back to San Diego Stadium once again. In an earth-shaking 45-17 victory, the Chargers up-rooted the Denver Broncos and re-planted them in last place in the Western Division. The victory gave San Diego a 6-7 record and made sure they would finish third--the sixth straight time.

<u>Houston</u>. But things changed a good bit at Houston. In the campaign finale, San Diego blew a 30-21 lead in the final minutes of the third quarter even though the Chargers' defense continued to do well. It snarled the Houston offense in the first half. Intercepted three Houston passes and recovered two fumbles. Bob Babich recovered both fumbles and ran one 27 yards for a touchdown. One of the interceptions set up Dennis Partee's 50-yard field goal. And <u>that</u> completed San Diego's 23-point second quarter.

Houston rallied, however, in the third quarter and San Diego couldn't match the rally. Oiler safety Ken Houston intercepted two successive Hadl passes for touchdowns. The Oilers picked up a 49-33 win and finished their season on a positive note.

<u>Looking back</u>.

Over-all, Babich was a dynamic middle-backer for San Diego. His role could be compared in importance to the role of the quarterback on offense. He set a Charger record for most tackles in a season (1971) with 194, a game average of 14. He had three fumble recoveries and three quarterback sacks, too.

Johnny Knapick said one time, *"Bob Babich was the greatest team-worker and team-leader I had the opportunity of coaching in my 30 years as head coach of Campbell Memorial High School."* Reflecting on his players, Knapick said, *"Bob Babich was always very dedicated to football."* he said, *"a well-liked individual who was never a discipline problem in school or on the field."*[4]

Another of Babich's high school coaches, Sloko Gill, was

talking about his former players. *"Bob Babich had real great speed, quickness, a real contact football player who gave 110% effort all the time. He was the best player I ever coached and surely without a doubt the greatest linebacker that ever played for Campbell Memorial High and in the Steel Valley Conference, for I have spent more than 50 years in area football."*[5]

Babich had both athletic ability and a sense of responsibility for the Chargers second line of defense. Those talents enabled him to become a celebrated linebacker, above and beyond other defensive players on the field. Behind all the glory though and like other linebackers, he had the hardest of assignments. Here is a summation of the requirements demanded of the position--and how Babich executed his duties while having such a great year:

> "We expect the linebacker to be strong enough to fight off the blocks of those big offensive linemen and quick enough to get to that ball carrier. He must also learn patience and be patient enough to wait and read, and alert enough to understand his keys, recognize the run and close the hole."

> "He must also be fast enough, once he reads the pass, to be able to cover the tight ends and the backs coming out of the backfield or, in the case of zone defense, to drop back into his area and to be able to cover any receiver who comes in there, and break up the pass or intercept it."

> "The basic difference between the defensive linemen and linebackers is that on the snap of the ball the linemen acts and then diagnoses; the linebacker, on the snap of the ball, diagnoses and then acts. The linebacker never guesses but rather waits for his key. It is far better for him to be a little hesitant than it is to react too quickly and do the wrong thing. Of course, this requires knowledge, confidence and self-control, and when you find people who have those qualities you're very, very fortunate and your defense is going to be a good defense."[6]

Babich became a hero at the middle-linebacker slot. Coming out of America's "rust belt" with skills steeltown fans could identify with, Babich became their symbol of achievement. The name "Babich" became a household name.

<u>New year, new schedule</u>.

The 1972 San Diego defensive unit was said to be a mixture of misfits and malcontents. Their reputation earned them the name "Dirty Dozen." Harland Svare, the San Diego coach, had recruited disgruntled but talented veterans from other teams in the NFL. This quick way of building for the future, according to Svare, was more practical than using the draft system year after year.

The defensive line filled up with the kind of player congenial to Svare's way of thinking. Ron East retained his position at tackle, while three veterans from other clubs joined him. Deacon Jones, former Ram, took a position at end. Lionel Aldridge came from Green Bay to play the other end. And Dave Costa, a refugee from Denver, played tackle next to Aldridge. When that tough threesome came to training camp, already dubbed as troublemakers, Jones nicknamed their defensive line "Harland's Hoodlums." Now <u>there</u> was a name everyone could identify in the mass of confusion.

"That's a good name," said Costa, who was raised in New York. *"When I was a kid, though, my crowd was actually pretty conservative. We only stole things beginning with 'A' --you know, a radio, a bicycle, a hubcap."*[7]

Suddenly, through the maze of team re-positioning, Bob found himself out of the middle-backer spot and placed at strong-side linebacker. He didn't particularly like playing outside: the middle was his favorite place. But it was a shift by Svare for the best interests of the club.

<u>49ers</u>. In their first game of the season, the Chargers made a lot of mistakes. The newly formed defense was out of sync. San Diego, taking on the toughest schedule in the NFL, lost their season opener. They made a really poor showing in a 34-3 loss to San Francisco before a vast crowd at Candlestick Park.

San Diego did everything wrong: fumbles (5), interceptions (4), penalties (11). It was one of those bad, bad days. Even then,

92

Babich and his teammates made some solid defensive stands that slowed the 49er offense.

Reporters asked Svare after the game if he saw anything good about the team's performance. *"Oh there were some things on defense,"* he said. *"But after we got so far behind it was like nothing we did was right."*

Broncos. Everything meshed the next week in San Diego Stadium. The Chargers bounced back, rolling to a 37-14 trouncing of the Broncos. Denver's Randy Montgomery rambled 94 yards on the opening kickoff for the game's first touchdown, and for some weird reason Coach Svare felt a sense of victory. *"I knew we would win when they returned the opening kickoff,"* said Svare. *"It's a funny thing to say, but that was just too much. Everything at first was too silly. The kickoff is what pulled us together."*[9]

John Hadl then hit for two touchdowns to meld the Chargers into a winning unit, and Mike Garrett had a fine day rushing. Also, with excellent line-backers like Babich and Pete Barnes, and linemen like Aldridge and Costa, the defense pulled itself together. They allowed the Broncos just 14 points, shutting them out in the second and third quarters. And the old adage that "defense wins" surfaced once more.

Raiders. The spectators jammed the Oakland (Alameda County) Coliseum. But they howled and groaned when George Blanda missed the game-winning field goal. So, tough luck. The tenacious San Diego defense put immense pressure on Oakland's field goal team. And Blanda's kick went wide right--with 1:10 left in the final period. Both teams settled for a 17-17 tie.

"It's a team thing," said Coach John Madden. *"You play out there for 60 minutes. It never comes down to one play or one person."*[10] But it was also the team work of Babich, Barnes, Deacon Jones, and others on San Diego's defense that confined Oakland to 90 yards rushing, preserving at least a tie.

Cowboys. After their 23-20 triumph over the Baltimore Colts the next week, San Diego's schedule turned into a rocky road. Even though the Chargers made a late comeback effort, they lost another close one--to the Dallas Cowboys by a 34-28 margin.

<u>Browns</u>. Then, came another last minute defeat for San Diego. The Chargers played at home in front of a packed house. And the Browns scored on a last-ditch effort very late in the game. Mike Phipps completed a touchdown pass to Frank Pitts: Cleveland won, 21-17.

Statistically, the Browns played lower-caliber football than the Chargers because "Harland's Hoodlums" mounted such strong defensive play. But San Diego also led the league in turnovers. That statistic alone would explain the Chargers' four straight losses before playing the Browns. Another factor that hurt San Diego was Babich's absence from the starting line up. He had been one of the Chargers' defensive kingpins all season.

"He didn't start for the first time in recent memory Monday night, and Harland Svare said it was because his right leg was dragging. The description seemed appropriate."[11]

The whole 1972 campaign was a difficult time for Babich. According to the medical diagnosis, he had been having trouble with that old knee injury. Babich had been replaced as San Diego's middle-linebacker. He played at the strong-side position because coach Svare felt that was where his talents would help the most. But Bob missed the glamour of being San Diego's middle-linebacker. That was the position that paid large sums of money. No small consideration! Babich knew it. The most publicized linebackers were Butkus, Lanier, and Curtis. And they became famous by doing their thing in the middle-backer spot. Babich was their equal in talent and smarts for the position.

Still, during summer camp at Irvine, Bob didn't complain about his plight on the Chargers' defense. He just accepted the change as a fact of life and was too much a professional to say anything. Bob didn't grouse about it as the campaign continued, but he was always open to <u>discuss</u> his new role as a defensive player.

"I'm getting used to it," he said. *"I'm learning how to play off certain blocks and how to read the different keys. It's not easy, though.....It's like trying to learn how to play football all over again."*[12] Bob didn't start in the Browns' game, because his

knee had been in pain, and he didn't practice that week, trying to give his knee a rest.

During the second half, Svare adjusted the San Diego defense and sent Babich in at the strong side. *"That's the best he's looked in a long time,"* said the coach afterward. *"He was moving around out there real good."*

"I felt better," said Babich. *"The rest definitely helped. Technically, I don't know what's wrong with the knee. All I know is that it's sore and it bothers me...It's frustrating. It's a nagging kind of injury."*[13] The injury was of much concern to Svare and the Chargers organization. With a 2-6-1 record, San Diego was looking toward the future, and that future involved Babich--wherever he played defense.

Some football experts thought Babich should have worn a set of shining armor, not a football uniform. In terms of stereotypes, Bob really did resemble a Roman gladiator. At times, ball carriers must have thought Babich had a spear in his possession. Over the previous two campaigns as middle-backer, Babich had made an amazing total of 367 tackles. That by itself could be the reason his knees got banged up.

Supposedly a future All-Pro middle-linebacker, Bob had the range, the strength, and the mobility. He also had a new coach with new ideas.

"Svare feels that his strongest linebacker should always line up opposite the tight end. And Babich is the strongest linebacker."[13]

"Some have questioned the switch, pointing out that Babich's number 60 isn't as visible as it once was. But that could have been a result of his knee injury or it could have been a simple case of not getting the opportunities outside you normally get in the middle."[14]

So Svare was pleased with the change and didn't plan to move Babich back to the middle. Babich continued to play, giving 110% effort, and wondering about his future in the NFL. *"My purpose is the same,"* he said. *"I want to play good football. And I want to be here when this losing turns around for us."* A bystander assured Bob that it would. *"I hope so."*[15] said Babich.

Chiefs. The next week, noisy Kansas City fans came to see San Diego upset the Chiefs in Arrowhead Stadium, 27-17. The Charger defense, with Babich in at full tilt, allowed Kansas City only seven first-period points. And it held them scoreless in the second quarter. That cushion enabled Hadl to stabilize San Diego's offense.

Raiders...again. As the season moved along, San Diego just could not break old behavior patterns. They blew a 19-14 fourth-quarter lead and lost to the Oakland Raiders Taking advantage of San Diego's missed field goal by Dennis Partee, and with 4 minutes left in the game, the Raiders beat the Chargers 21-19. They clinched the Western Division Championship and an NFL playoff spot for the fifth time in six years.

Here again, statistically, the Chargers won the battle because of solid defense but lost the war in total points. Babich played his best! In the campaign finale, Pittsburgh beat San Diego and won its first NFL title of any sort after 40 years of frustration. Art Rooney handed out cigars in the Pittsburgh locker room after his Steelers won by 24-2.

"It took a long time, but it was worth it," said the white-haired, 71 year-old club owner. *"I'm not jumping up and down because that's not the way I am. But inside I'm bubbling like a volcano."*[16]

After Cleveland disposed of the New York Jets 26-10, Pittsburgh had to defeat the Chargers in order to finish ahead of Cleveland in the AFC Central Division. Pittsburgh's defense came through in the "must win" situation. It forced seven Charger turnovers. Also, it held San Diego in bad field position and shut down their ground game.

"I've seen and played against a lot of Steeler teams, and this is the best Pittsburgh team I've ever seen,"[17] said Coach Svare.

By comparison, the San Diego defense--led by Dave Costa and Bob Babich had just as good a day as their opponents. The offensive statistics were close to equal, but the score was not. *"The Steelers were held in check most of the game by a San Diego defensive charge lead by tackle Dave Costa and linebacker Bob Babich."*[18]

Although they lost more games than they won, they played like champions. They didn't give up for one minute along the way. Like Vince Lombardi said, "Winning is not everything--but <u>making the effort</u> to win is."[19]

Bob Babich - Courtesy of Miami (O.) University Sports Information Dept.

BACK TO OHIO

Bob Babich was thrilled to be traded to the Cleveland Browns just ten days before the start of the 1973 regular season. While still in training with San Diego in late summer, Bob anticipated and welcomed the change over to Cleveland.

"I'm very excited," he said. *"I hope that I'm worth everything that they've given up for me."*[1]

The Browns gave up a first round draft pick in 1974, a second pick the next year, and a fourth-round choice in 1975 to lure Babich away from San Diego.

"He's the big answer to help us against the run," said Coach Nick Skorich. *"With Babich at middle linebacker, the rest of the things will fall into place."*[2]

Coach Skorich had spent 39 days cutting the deal that pried Babich loose from the Chargers. But after the deal, Skorich saw Babich as solving a long-time middle-backer problem for the Browns. He would ease the pressure at the defensive ends.

"Joe Jones and Les Sims have been coming along and with good support inside, they can be more reckless against the pass," Skorich said. *"Babich will be even more effective behind Walter Johnson and Jerry Sherk at the defensive tackles. And if you control the running game, you're not always in a precarious situation on second down."*[3]

But, of course, Babich felt he was back where he belonged: at middle linebacker. *"I think I've wasted the last year and a half playing the outside for San Diego. I'm better suited playing sideline to sideline. It's a little dull on the outside."*[4]

Babich believed that, with his experience, he had been San Diego's best middle-linebacker. He thought so even after the Chargers swapped for the eccentric Tim Rossovich from the Philadelphia Eagles. *"But the coaches didn't think so,"* said Babich. *"I didn't get along with Rossovich,"* he continued. *"He's a nice guy, but we're completely different personalities. I don't set myself on fire."*[5]

The fact was: Babich lived a more conservative personal life than Rossovich. Rossovich had a reputation for unusual tastes--

like chewing great wads of tobacco and consuming beer <u>bottles</u>.

Skorich appreciated real talent, and his thinking was in line with Babich's. *"We studied films of Babich and he looked completely lost on the outside,"* said Skorich. *"He doesn't have quite the quickness to go deep out there. But he still does the 40 under five seconds and that's faster than any of our middle linebackers now."*[6]

Skorich admitted the cost for Babich was high, giving up a number of draft choices. *"We had to pay a steep price, but he fills a major need, one we had to solve,"* he said. *"We've been looking year after year after year in the draft for a middle linebacker and never got one....We might have drafted one next year and still not known for sure if he could do it. We figured why not give up the choice now and get a qualified man? We felt it was the best way to solve the problem."*[7]

Defensive end Bob Briggs, Babich's roommate at San Diego before Bob went to Cleveland, agreed with the coaches' thoughts. *"Bob is fantastic,"* said Briggs. *"He's hard-nosed, a 110 per cent player, and a full speed hitter. The offensive backs don't drive him. He sends them over backwards ....I definitely think he's going to be a helper for us. He'll be the strongest guy on our team. He bench presses 435 pounds, he's so massive in his upper body."*[8]

Babich had met with Briggs when Cleveland played in San Diego the previous year. *"I told him if the Browns really needed a middle-linebacker I'd be more than happy to come to Cleveland,"* said Babich. *"I'd watched the Browns since I was five years old. They always were my favorite team. It's sorta weird how things have worked out a year later."*[9]

After undergoing a physical, Babich started practice immediately with the Browns. Getting himself ready for the regular season opener with the Baltimore Colts. And the Browns won their opener with the Colts at Cleveland Stadium. Their defense shut down Baltimore's running game most of the time, putting heavy pressure on Bert Jones, the Colts' quarterback. The pass rush made the secondary coverage a lot easier in Cleveland's 24-14 triumph.

"I feel that the defense did a great job," Nick said. *"The*

offense got us into trouble but the defense bailed us out."[9]

Mike Phipps carried the burden on offense for Cleveland. He rushed for 55 yards and threw a touchdown pass to Frank Pitts. Babich shared middle-linebacker duties with starter Billy Andrews. The coaches were even considering putting Babich in as the regular the next week.

"It could happen," replied the coach. *"Babich has been coming along well. He's picking up our system. He's very quick. You probably noticed how he got the passer on that one blitz.*"[10]

Babich wanted to be number one as the middle man, and he was working his way up for the tough schedule ahead. *"Right now I'm not even third best," Babich said, "but I'm working on it.*"[11]

Babich did his thing--working on the Colts. During the second half, Baltimore only made three first downs, and one of those was on a penalty. The other two came late in the game when it didn't matter much to the Browns. *"I was a little nervous when I first went in. I felt like a rookie,"* said the new middle-backer. *"I didn't play well for the first few series. But as the game progressed I felt more at ease. I haven't played middle-linebacker for two years.*"[12]

Babich actually played longer than he'd thought he would in place of Billy Andrews. *"I knew I was gonna play a little, but I thought it would only be for a few series. I thought he wanted to just give me a little playing time.*"[13] Babich said.

Coach Skorich smiled when asked about Babich starting against a tough Pittsburgh team the following week. Skorich said, *"He looked about ready.*"[14]

Babich sparkled in front of the home town boosters from Youngstown. And he brought 74,300 fans to their feet when he sacked Colts' quarterback Bert Jones in the fourth period. It was a linebacker blitz, throwing the Colts for a 10-yard loss.

<u>Giants</u>. The turning point in Cleveland's 12-10 victory over the Giants was their defense.

The defense stalled New York's offense several times. With such a superb defensive effort, the Browns ran 74 offensive plays as compared to the New Yorkers' 45.

"The defense is the story of this game," declared Skorich. *"It gave us the shutout we had to have the second half. That's why we gave all of them game balls....Yes, Bob Babich did well at middle-linebacker. It was a fine team effort."*[15]

"We played reckless ball," said Babich. *"Recklessness is not gambling. When you read your keys and commit yourself, you commit full go. You don't worry about making a lot of mistakes. Last week we were hesitating."*[16]

<u>Dolphins</u>. The Browns played as well as they could, and their defense received special praise against Miami. Miami won by 17-9, however, and Cleveland lost a hard fought battle.

Babich said: *"There were no fancy plays. Just head on head. In a game like that something had to break and unfortunately it broke against us."*[17] Mercury Morris raced 70 yards to set up the Miami Dolphins' go-ahead touchdown in the third quarter. It was Miami's big play of the day. Then the Dolphins picked off a Mike Phipps pass in the fourth period, setting up the game clincher. *"I thought <u>we</u> could win it, 12-10."* said Babich.

Coach Skorich blamed the Browns' loss on an illegal-motion penalty that hurt at a crucial time. The Browns were gaining momentum until the infraction. Cleveland's defense did a great job in holding Paul Warfield to one pass reception. He was Miami's best receiver. What really hurt was that the Dolphins, after getting by a tough Browns team, went ahead later to win Super-Bowl VIII.

<u>Steelers</u>. When Cleveland and Pittsburgh met towards the end of the campaign, it turned out to be a typical rowdy rock'em, sock'em ballgame. From the sea of crunches and tangles, the Browns surfaced as a 21-16 victor. But Phipps was not impressed with the victory. He wasn't pleased that Pittsburgh beat Cleveland in every statistic but the scoreboard.

Babich disagreed with Phipps' opinion about the game. *"Stats mean nothing,"* Babich said. *"The name of the game is to keep them out of the end zone. Except for their first touchdown drive, that's what we did."*[18]

"The hand injury which forced Pittsburgh quarterback Terry Hanratty from the game early in the first quarter was not a break for the Browns." said Babich. *"After seeing their*

third string quarterback, Joe Gilliam. I think he may have a faster release than either Terry Bradshaw or Hanratty," he continued. *"He played like a veteran. He didn't get rattled. He had full control of the team at all times. He's going to be a great leader. And he's very mobile."*[19]

Two weeks later, Coach Skorich was handing out praise, *"Bob Babich had become the catalyst of our defense."*[20] It was a defense that <u>could</u> become the greatest in the NFL, according to Babich.

On Tuesday of that week, the Cleveland Touchdown Club chose Babich and cornerback Clarence Scott co-winners of the Defensive Player Of The Year award. *"I'm very honored...I'm very excited about it,"* said Babich. *"It's a tremendous honor and I feel gratified. They [the Browns] paid a high price for me and I wanted to be worth it."*[21]

Skorich applauded both Babich and Scott as fine selections! *"Babich is the catalyst of our defense. It was no coincidence that our defense became really good when he came to Cleveland. He's the main reason why John Garlington and Charlie Hall are having such great years as outside linebackers."*[22]

"The defense here can become the best in the NFL. We could play together as a unit another seven years and become like the Packers or Giants defenses of old," Babich added. *"Playing together with these guys is a tremendous experience. It snowballs into an emotional thing. One of my biggest thrills had to be stopping both Pittsburgh and Kansas City with fourth and three inches."*[23]

"It's a typical Cleveland team."[24] Babich continued. *"I've followed them for years and they always come through. It's been the same this year. We were down a little bit earlier, but we never gave up."*

<u>Bengals</u>. In the game coming up, the Browns would play the Bengals at Cincinnati, and the Bengals had a high-powered offense. *"It's going to be another tough one,"* said Babich. *"It may be the toughest one yet."*[25] It <u>was</u> a tough one. Mostly for the Browns. The Bengals, first place in the Central Division, defeated the Browns 34-17.

<u>Rams</u>. In the season finale the next week, Cleveland suffered a second straight loss. The Los Angeles Rams, NFC Western Division champs, won over Cleveland by 30-17. The Rams scored an amazing 27 of their 30 points in the first half. Cleveland couldn't catch up even though their defense did an outstanding job in the second half.

Thus, Cleveland finished the season with a 7-5-2 record and third place in the AFC Central Division. Coincidence: on that same Sunday, running back O. J. Simpson of the Buffalo Bills rushed for 200 yards against the New York Jets. He broke Jim Brown's single-season NFL rushing record with 2,003 yards.

And Babich earned his place on the Brown's honor roll, having had such a great first year with the team.

<u>1974: What goes around.</u>

To start the 1974 campaign, Babich signed a three-year contract with the Browns. He would be a key figure in Cleveland's defense. *"I'm very pleased about it."* said Babich when reached in his off season home in San Diego. *"No, I never really considered the World Football League... I wanted to play in Cleveland. I was happy when I was traded to the Browns last year and I want to stay with the team."*[26]

Bob did not have a "no-cut" clause in his contract and it was not even a part of the negotiations. *"That didn't concern me."* he said. *"I have enough confidence in my ability. I don't need a no cut."* Babich was looking forward to the start of the campaign. *"I anticipate a very exciting team."* he said. *"Hopefully, we'll get back on top in our division and make the playoffs....I hope to be a part of the Browns for a long time. Five, six, seven-- maybe eight years. I love football and want to play as long as I possibly can."*[27]

At one time Bob was considering Cleveland for his permanent home. *"There is a good possibility that we'll move to Cleveland,"* he said. *"It depends on a number of things... I plan to come in several weeks before the start of training camp to get used to the heat and the humidity. I have started workouts, running and playing racquetball."*[28]

Bob had been exceptional the year before. Even more exceptional, he played in pain with a reoccurring knee injury. He was one of the most dedicated athletes who ever played pro football. *"The knee isn't bothering me,"*[29] he said. *"I've had it checked regularly and everything seems fine. It certainly should be a lot better than last year."*

During the 1973 campaign, Babich had proved to be a nose-to-nose middle-backer, very tough against the run. He also left a big impression on Browns' fans when he made a 48-yard run-back with an interception. It was the longest of the year for the Browns, and it came against the defending Super Bowl champion Dolphins. Babich pushed himself on a consistent basis to be better each year. *"Now I know the system and am more accustomed to the people around me,"* he said. *"It should help all of us."*[30]

Babich responded to questions about Cleveland's new defensive coordinator, Richie McCabe. *"I don't believe we'll be as conservative,"* he said. *"I believe we'll do more gambling and be more reckless. That can cause the other team to make mistakes."*

Babich's lawyer friend, Don McGrath, handled contract negotiations for him with the Browns. *"He is a personal friend and comes from a very respected law firm,"* Bob explained. *"He handles all my investments. I'm very pleased with the contract."*

Art Modell was pleased to have Babich join the Browns. *"We are delighted that Bob has seen fit to commit himself to our organization for years to come,"*[31] said the Cleveland owner. *"His presence in the middle of the defense is most reassuring. He was a prime factor in the improvement of our defensive performance in 1973."*

<u>A new season.</u>

One of the most difficult tasks for a pro football organization is to build a winning team. If the team starts losing for some unforeseen circumstance, the season becomes a series of frustrations. The Browns started feeling frustrated after their devastating first game. They lost to the Cincinnati Bengals 33-7.

Cleveland's offense could not get going long enough even to give the defense a rest!

Houston. In week #2, things improved a little. The Browns beat an inept Houston Oilers' club at the Stadium by 20-7. Cleveland was an improved ball team, but they still didn't take advantage of turnovers their strong defense gave them. Cleveland's defense recovered three fumbles, intercepted three passes, and stopped Houston on a fourth and one.

"We did more blitzing and more stunting," said Skorich. *"I was pleased with the work against the running game. The Oilers came here with the leading ground gainer [Ronnie Coleman] in our conference."*[32]

The linebacker and defensive linemen coordinated well with the defensive backfield, limiting Houston's total offense to 168 yards. *"We're starting to get our rhythm,"* said Babich. *We're getting more and more fluid. I think we have just about made up for the time we lost."* Babich described Houston's fumbles and their giving the ball away on pass interceptions. *"We played aggressive defense and forced them into mistakes,"* he said. *"And then we capitalized on most of them."*[33]

The offensive line, anchored by Bob Demarco, played like a cohesive force, opening holes in Houston's odd-man front. But no wild celebration erupted in the Browns' dressing room. After the win over a mediocre Oilers team, the Browns felt just a dull sense of mild gratification.

Cardinals. When the game ended the following week in St. Louis, the Browns tried to figure out what went wrong. They lost 29-7 to the Cardinals. The players spoke in generalities of poor execution, breaks, and big plays. It seemed like a reoccurring nightmare from the very first loss against Cincinnati, with no cure-all in sight.

"I don't have the slightest idea what's wrong," said Babich. *"I just know we have to keep hanging in there. It will take just a couple of breaks to get us back in contention and those breaks will come."*[34]

Coach Skorich gave his honest opinion of the loss that left Cleveland at 1-2 on the season. *"We did a poor job offensively,"* he said. *"We've got to get better execution out of the offense.*

We've got to move the ball."[35] Nobody mentioned the fact that the "Big Red" Cardinals had a tough physical team who forced Cleveland into costly errors.

Bengals. Two weeks later, 70,897 fans packed Cleveland Stadium. Most of them were disgusted when the Browns lost-- for the fourth time in five games--to the Bengals, 34-24. This time the Browns' defense sagged to a totally non-productive mass and became a chapter in a mystery story. Their defense, not playing up to form, gave up 452 total yards and let quarterback Ken Anderson connect on three touchdown passes. *"We've got to do something,"* said a puzzled Skorich. *"The defense let us down."*

"We're making mistakes, and I don't know why," said Babich. *"The personnel is good and we haven't had that many changes from last year when the defense was decent."*[36]

Defensive end Nick Roman mused, *"I'm as perplexed as anybody. I'm tired about this talk about pass rush. Eleven people have to do their job."*[37]

The offense was given credit for playing good enough to win. The defense was criticized for making the same mistake twice. Babich admitted, *"The defense knew what it had to do when the Browns pulled within three. The big thing was to stop them and try to get the turnover,"* he said.

Babich did recover a Charlie Joiner fumble: that gave his statement credibility. Unfortunately, the referee had ruled the recovery an infraction after the whistle. *"It was a quick whistle,"*[38] Babich tried to explain. *"I thought I had the ball."*

The offense didn't show any upturn in emotions after the encounter, either. But they got, if any, the praise.

Steelers. "You Live With Your Mistakes." That was the motto for the Browns after they lost 20-16 to the Pittsburgh Steelers. It was an upset bid at Three Rivers Stadium. Chuck Knoll, head coach of Pittsburgh said, *"The Browns gave us a big scare in an all out affair with both teams playing hard nose football."*[39] Football experts had made Cleveland 15-point underdogs. Still, the Browns apparently <u>tried</u> to beat the predictions.

In the fourth period they were marching downfield. But

Mike Phipps, under defensive pressure, rushed a late-quarter pass to Hugh McKinnis. Glen Edwards intercepted it to stall the drive--and to end Cleveland's chances. It was the same old story: time ran out.

Bob Babich was the defensive standout for the Browns. He made the most tackles of anyone on either team: eight solos and nine assists.

<u>Bad news tally</u>.

So Cleveland sports fans were looking for a ray of hope. Almost any ray, any hope! And the Cleveland Browns pulled a fourth-period upset victory over the Denver Broncos. After the Browns defeated Denver 23-21, a group of excited reporters encircled owner Art Modell. Modell congratulated the beleaguered Skorich, who had been under attack from "outsiders" while the club lost four straight.

Like the team leader he was, Babich set a positive example for his teammates by reassuring them that the team <u>would win</u> this time. Bob was consistently positive, especially throughout the losing streak. But the Broncos made a last minute surge that kept Babich on his toes. He didn't want this one to slip through Cleveland's hands.

"We had stopped them before and I knew we could do it again," said Babich. He was especially pleased with the victory against Johnson. *"He's probably the best, and he's for sure the smartest,"*[40] said Babich. *"He kept us off balance with his play calling. He did a lot of different things."*

Oh, the beat went on throughout the last half of the NFL season. Through it all Babich played like a champion, an eternal optimist. He never gave in to defeat, although the Browns won only twice more that year, finishing with a 4-10-0 record.

WHILE YOU'RE AHEAD

Babich was having trouble with his knee in 1975. He really needed to give his knee some healing time. So, after the fourth game of the regular season, he gave way to rookie middle-linebacker Dick Ambrose. After the Browns lost John Garlington to knee surgery, however, they called on Bob to play outside linebacker midway into the season. Bob always worked hard at football and was open to new suggestions from his coaches.

"The transition of different coaching concepts confuses some players, but Bob is a very willing person in taking on new ideas and is a hard worker,"[1] said Walt Corey, linebacker coach.

"It was hard to come back and adjust to middle-linebacker in 1973 after what I call my 'lost' years on the outside at San Diego," said Babich. *"If I didn't enjoy football, I don't think I'd be here....It's not worth the time and sacrifices, and the pain you go through, to play this game just for money. If you don't enjoy what you're doing, you're wasting your time and everyone else's."*[2]

Babich spoke of a winning season in front of the Cleveland Touchdown Club. Its members were asking questions about the Browns' losing their first four games of the season. Bob always had great confidence in himself and the Browns football team.

"I think we'll finish better than 7-7," commented Babich. *"We're going to show people we are a good football team and capable of doing the job we're supposed to be doing."*[3]

The veteran linebacker could not put his finger on any one folly that had caused the Browns not to jell as winners. *"Unfortunately, we're not playing the type of football we're capable of,"* he explained. *"But it's a little too early to give up on the Browns. We are not giving up on ourselves.... We have better material here than at any time since I've been with the Browns. At every position we have a sounder football team than in either of the last two seasons. That's what makes this so hard to understand....We need a win--by one or 40 points, it doesn't matter--and we can be on our way,"* he said.

Although the coaching staff came under criticism, Babich respected the coaches and held them in high esteem. *"I think every coach on the club is very well qualified,"* he said firmly. *"I've been in pro football seven years and this is the best coaching staff I've had."*

"We're well prepared," he continued. *"The coaches are doing their job. You can't really blame the system or the coverage. We just can't put our finger on the problem."*[4]

After the Browns blew a lead in a 40-10 loss to the Houston Oilers, the defense had taken most of the blame. Babich spoke truthfully but with a definite point of view about the deteriorating situation. *"Once you get a lead, you're suppose to protect it. We're not as bad as we've looked the last three weeks. We've just got to put it together. I hope we do it soon,"* he concluded.

At any rate, the Browns faltered during the second half of the campaign. They just couldn't put the needed ingredients together for a winning year. Babich's predictions and insights didn't prove to be true until 1976, when the Browns bounced back with a 9-5 win-loss mark.

Determined to win.

When summer camp began in 1976, most people were uncertain about how well the Browns would perform during the regular season. Most football writers picked them to finish at the bottom of the Central Division. With a nucleus of veterans from the catastrophic season of 1975, the players grew more and more determined to have a successful year. Their camaraderie held a serious undertone of motivation.

Jets. Sure enough, the Browns proved they were winners in a 38-17 drubbing of the New York Jets on opening day. The same familiar names were in the Browns' line-up: Mike Phipps, Greg Pruitt, Cleo Miller, Tom Deleone, Doug Dieken, and Paul Warfield. Walter Johnson, Jerry Sherk, Clarence Scott, and Bob Babich made up the foundation for Cleveland's "pillar of strength" defense.

Steelers. The pillar wobbled a bit the following week. The Browns dropped a 31-14 decision to Pittsburgh. And Steelers' fans were delighted to see Cleveland self-destruct. The Browns were their own worst enemies. Their mistakes lost a game in which the Steelers really were not the dominant force.

Cleveland had earned the reputation of being a first-half team. They scored all their points in the second period, playing brilliant football. They also continued to make costly errors. Still, they were down only three points (17-14) during the third period. At defense things were not flawless, either. Babich dropped a sure interception and missed out on a touchdown run. He couldn't believe that he'd dropped a sure thing. Believe it: it happened.

<u>Broncos</u>. In the next game, some viewers saw a replay of the preceding week. The Browns took a humiliating 44-13 loss from the Broncos. And Browns' general manager Pete Hadhazy threatened to make some sudden personnel changes after the game.

"There are a few players on this team who don't belong in this league,"[5] an angry Hadhazy stormed in the locker room. *"We're going to get rid of the players who are hurting us, helping us lose games....We made a lot of mistakes and we didn't have the poise to come back when we were on the two-yard line and didn't score. If the score was 17-14 at the half, we would have won the game. This team is too good to get blown out by a mediocre Denver team. And you can quote me. A mediocre Denver team."*[6]

Head coach Forrest Gregg was disgruntled with the loss, too. He said, *"We didn't play very well. I really don't know the reason....Maybe, it's because we were so high last week. Whatever it was, we carried on just as we finished in Pittsburgh. Maybe it was a letdown."*[7]

Brian Sipe brought the Browns back for a second-quarter touchdown. Then late in the period, the Browns got a break: Bob Babich recovered an Armstrong fumble. Quickly the Browns moved into field goal range. But Don Cockroft blew a 28-yard attempt, and that wasted opportunity slowed Cleveland's momentum.

<u>Steelers...again</u>. In the second meeting of the Browns and Steelers, many fans let their emotions run free. It was an interstate grudge match in Cleveland Stadium. And the Browns

finally got their revenge with an 18-16 win. The lakefront team turned potential into performance with a fine running game and passing attack. Nobody spoke about it much, but four important Don Cockroft field goals accounted for most of Cleveland's points. Regardless, this victory gave Cleveland hopes of staying in the division race.

<u>Chargers</u>. Elation ran through the stands two weeks later. Cleveland came from three points down to defeat a powerful San Diego team. The fans were soaking wet on a rainy day, but happy about the outcome. The defense claimed some recognition in a second-half stand. They held the Chargers to just one field goal, a comeback from their second-quarter collapse.

Whatta you know! it was Cleveland's third victory in a row. They would have to play Cincinnati the next week and Houston the week after. But the Browns had a 4-3 record halfway through the season. That sure was an improvement compared with an 0-7 mark at the same time a year earlier. Cleveland's defensive unit deserved a lot of credit for the turn-around.

The Browns' strategy was to give the Charger offense access to short pass completions. Dan Fouts of San Diego settled for the sure short passes, but they made his team vulnerable to defeat. As a result, the Browns' linebackers shut down the San Diego offense. Fouts was throwing to five different running backs or concentrating on the tight end. So, Cleveland linebackers'--Bob Babich, Gerald Irons, and Charlie Hall--knew what they had to do. Babich made 14 tackles, Hall 10, and Irons 4. It came to a total of 28 tackles in 49 plays.

"We had to be on our toes today," said Babich. *"Anytime the defense plays well, you know the linebackers have to play a good game."*[8] The major defensive concern was how to keep Charlie Joiner from the deep pass.

<u>Bengals</u>. "Next week" arrived on schedule, and the Browns faced a rugged Cincinnati defense inside the 10-yard line. The Bengals stopped Cleveland short four times. The Browns got only six points on Cockroft's field goals. Result: loss, again. Bob Babich broke his hand early in the first quarter, but he continued to play. Knowing Bob, "Mr. Desire," everybody figured the injury would not sideline him for the season.

Oilers. With a solid defensive effort, however, the Browns pulled it together the next week in a decisive 21-7 win over the Houston Oilers. That game marked the first in a series of five straight wins. Oh, those Browns football fans were whooping it up during the latter part of the season.

With a 14-7 score in favor of Cleveland, Houston still had visions of tying the score late in the fourth period. They wanted to throw the game into overtime after Cockroft's missed field goal. But Babich, playing smart football, grabbed a John Hadl pass deflected by a Browns' free safety. Playing with that broken bone in his left hand, Babich returned the ball 21 yards to the Oilers 40-yard line.

From there, Brian Sipe directed a six-play drive. Runs by Mike Pruitt and Larry Poole, plus passes to Oscar Roan, led to the touchdown and an end to the scoring.

Eagles. While the defense made another contribution to the Browns' victory march, Bob Babich succeeded in his own personal goals. He bested his counterpart, Bill Bergey, during Cleveland's 24-3 thumping of Philadelphia. *"The only way you get recognition is to play better than their star,"* said Babich.

Philadelphia had obtained middle linebacker Bill Bergey through a trade agreement with the Cincinnati Bengals. The trade mostly involved future draft choices. After the triumph over San Diego, Babich looked at his statistics sheet on tackles made.

"Nine solo tackles and 11 assisted, not bad," said Babich.

"Who did that? somebody asked.

"I did,"[9] Babich smiled.

Bergey made eight solo tackles and four assisted. Babich had came up with a personal triumph. During the course of the encounter, the Browns' star linebacker managed to pick off an Eagles pass. It was Bob's second interception inside two weeks. It was awkward at that, with his left hand in a cast. Babich would have had three interceptions to his credit, but the one he returned for a touchdown four weeks earlier was called back on a penalty.

"Philadelphia was tougher than I thought," said Babich. *"They're coming. It was close up to the fourth quarter."*[10]This

was the first time the Browns had had <u>fun</u> on defense since their opener with the New York Jets.

<u>Tampa Bay</u>. A week later, the Browns sailed by the Buccaneers. The win at Tampa Bay gave them a 24-7 victory and a tie for second place with Pittsburgh in the AFC Central Division. Babich made eight unassisted tackles to tighten up the defense.

<u>Dolphins</u>. Through the cold and snow, satisfied fans watched until the final second of the Dolphins vs. Browns game. They saw the Browns make a great, late defensive stand to defeat the Miami Dolphins, 17-13. Head coach Forest Gregg was very, <u>very</u> happy to capture such a victory. Fan support rose to its highest level for the year.

"This is a wonderful feeling,"[11] declared Gregg. *"The defense did a super job, one beautiful job....And so did the special teams. We felt we had to stop their kick returns and we did."*

Browns players wouldn't have predicted an 8-4 mark during training camp, but the coaches had a hunch that they would be able to finish better than .500. The Browns were still tied for second place with the Steelers. Both clubs stayed one game behind division leader Cincinnati. At this point, the Browns had wild card playoff hopes in mind. It was still a mathematical possibility. If the Browns concentrated, they could defeat their next two foes and make it to the playoffs.

<u>Houston</u>. Well, the lakefront team did concentrate the following week. The Browns finished their home game season with a 13-10 win over the Houston Oilers. And it was a game of strong emotions for the winners. Sometimes Cleveland earned costly penalties. They bobbled and fumbled and gave up turnovers. The game was a nail-biter, and the score was close right down to the wire. But in the final 1:38 of the fourth period, the Cleveland defense came through in the clutches and iced the victory.

John Hadl came off the bench to replace quarterback Dan Pastorini. *"We were moving the ball,"* said Pastorini. *"I thought we had a good chance to get down for at least a field goal."*[12]

It was a totally unexpected situation for Hadl. Coach Bum Phillips wanted to use both quarterbacks on the next play, but

114

Hadl thought he was finished for the day. *"Hadl threw a pass toward wide receiver Earl Thomas. Charlie Hall intercepted for Cleveland, but it was Babich who made the play."*[13]

"Babich tipped it," said Hadl. *"He got just the tip of a finger on it. It was a great defensive play."*[14] Then Cleveland ran out the clock, and once more the defense was allotted first place in the dressing room victory songs.

<u>Closing the season</u>.

Thus, for the Browns to make the playoffs, they would have to defeat their final opponent of the season: Kansas City. As fortune would have it, the Browns fell in defeat to the Kansas City Chiefs. They found themselves with a third-place spot in the AFC Central Division. The Cincinnati Bengals were in first place, ahead of Pittsburgh. But they lost to the Western Division champions, the Oakland Raiders. And Oakland advanced to crush the Minnesota Vikings 32-14, in Super Bowl XI.

A big part of Cleveland's 9-5 winning record was its defensive unit. It was a unit made up of athletes with outstanding courage, senses of responsibility, and loyalty to their team. Some stood out a little more than others and received a little more recognition. Coach Gregg spoke of Bob Babich's outstanding comeback year as Cleveland's middle linebacker.

"I've never seen him play better. He did a fine job on both pass coverage and the run,"[15] said Gregg.

Bob reflected on the season, *"I didn't do anything special in the off-season to get my job back. I had confidence in my ability, and knew I could play the football I was capable of if I was healthy."*

Babich was motivated by the difficulties his team faced in that 1975 season. *"It sits in your stomach the whole year, and it works on you,"*[16] he said. *"Then you read the pre-season predictions, and see everyone saying we'll be last again. You start thinking, 'We'll show 'em.'"*

Bob spent the 1977 and 1978 seasons, his last two years in football, with the Cleveland Browns' specialty teams. Then after his 1978 retirement, he accepted a position with the Bank of America in San Diego, a position he had held during off-seasons. A position he still holds today.

Photos of Sharon Steel Corp., Sharon, PA. Taken by Ron "Tank" Rotunno.

EPILOGUE: TODAY

Game by game, season after season, we've looked at three men from small Ohio high schools. Their football origins: the Steel Valley Conference. How they played the game. The memories of their heroism that people cherish "back home." All three were dedicated to something larger than themselves--to the greater good of their teams, to their own concepts of personal excellence. Their dreams of a college education. Their families...the future.

They played whenever they could, even when they were injured, sick, or when they drew assignments they didn't care for. Despite numerous set-backs, they never quit. We've known of coaches, hoping to develop character, who kept this motto in their offices:

"It isn't whether you've won or lost,

But how you played the game."

And that's true as far as it goes. The whole truth is that "how" is actually everything...game or no game. Those who are honest, who are determined to do their best--to excel if possible-- ultimately <u>become</u> winners in any field they enter. Whether they play or not.

Two of the men we've read about were tempted to drop out before they finished high school. It's a common temptation. One knew almost from the beginning that he wanted "life after football." All three went on to college and, later, played professional football. Not one of the three is in the Football Hall of Fame. At least, not yet. Not one of the three wears a Super Bowl ring. But they know and we know they are winners.

All three are concerned today about young people, especially the young ones tempted by easy answers. The ones our high school athletics programs exploit frequently under the guise of "school spirit." The ones who have not yet learned to look beyond today's glitter and gold chains.   Vince Lombardi said it right:

"Lately, in our society, it seems that we have sympathy
only for the losers and misfits. Let us also <u>cheer</u> for the

doers and the winners. The zeal to be first in everything has always been American, to win and to win and to win. Not everyone can be a winner all the time, but every-one can make that effort, that personal commitment to excellence and to victory."[1]

Mel Triplett today is a retired supervisor from the City of Toledo, Ohio where he lives. Four of his 15 children played football for Toledo Scott High School: two at fullback, one at tight-end and wide receiver, one at line-backer. All his children finished high school. One is a registered nurse. One is still in college. Mel enjoys playing with his grandchildren, telling them of his experiences with the New York Giants.

He is a quiet man, almost an introvert, but he is rightfully proud of his achievements and awards. If you asked him, he would tell you he'd "do it all over again." Mel is a Baptist minister. In addition, he supervises his own landscaping business. He speaks frequently to parents and church groups, emphasizing the need for their children to get the best education they can.

Bill Triplett worked in employee relations for General Motors, Packard Division, quite a few years before retiring. Three of his children (two boys and a girl) completed their college educations and are living in St. Louis. Bill is back in the Youngstown area now, counseling inner-city young people at the Needle's Eye Christian Mission. His message to youngsters is <u>anti-drugs, anti-alcohol, and anti-smoking</u>. He has seen their effects and cautions young people to Beware!

Bill stays in good physical condition, keeps his weight at about 218 lbs.--his playing weight with the Cardinals. He loves football to this day and believes it gave him self-confidence. Since his 1964 illness, he has believed the Good Lord gave him a purpose in life, a blessing--enabling him both to return to pro football and to develop speaking skills. The public speaking career he began in St. Louis still keeps him busy. He has spoken frequently to churches, school groups, and at sports banquets-- wherever and whenever he's needed.

His values? He believes that a person's <u>family</u> still should come first in everyone's life. He believes young people need three strong anchors for their lives: religious faith, family, and as much education as they can get. His youngest sister, Jacqueline White, describes him today: *"Bill is a kind-hearted person, soft-spoken. He wears a smile and always has a kind word for everybody."*

Throughout his football career, Bob Babich devoted himself to being the best middle-linebacker he could possibly be. He was always committed to a vision of excellence, and the values he held made him a natural team leader. Some of his values came from early childhood training. Some from the coaches who taught him how to play football. Together, they became part of what people call "character." Those values, in turn, like those of Mel and Bill Triplett, have became part of a football tradition. One of Ohio's best football traditions: that of the Steel Valley Conference.

Today, Bob Babich is a bank manager in San Diego's Bank of America. He spends a great deal of time working with the San Diego March of Dimes and the National Cancer Society. Through the San Diego Juvenile Probation Department, he works in their homes with troubled young people on a one-to-one basis—those who need counsel and positive role models. He also works with young people through the NFL Alumni Association and the National Football Foundation. He's also active in work with youngsters in the Special Olympics. Beginning in the fall of 1991, he was to begin broadcasting football games for both San Diego State and the University of San Diego. On December 6, 1994, he was inducted into the National Football Foundation and College Hall of Fame.

Mel and Bill Triplett and Bob Babich: three NFL football players from the same high school conference in Ohio. They still remember and treasure the camaraderie, the "team spirit," that develops when players play the game full tilt, when they give their best individually. They know the <u>will to win</u>, to excel, is a quality that endures long after the games are over.

High school football provided a stepping stone for them into college and professional football. All of them learned to play the game in the Steel Valley Conference. People in the Steel Valley are proud of all three.

END NOTES

END NOTES

Chapter I: From the Delta

1. Tuckner, Howard N. "Gridiron Softer Than Cotton Field." New York _Times_. November 6, 1956.
2. Ibid.   3. Ibid.   4. Ibid.
5. Ibid.   6. Ibid.   7. Ibid.
8. Ibid.
9. Toledo _Blade_, Oct 31, 1954. Sports Information Department, Toledo University, Toledo, Ohio.
10. Cuddy, Jack. "Best Since Nagurski?" United Press press release. October 27, 1956.
11. Ibid.   12. Ibid.
13. Ibid.   14. Ibid.   15. Ibid.
16. Ibid.   17. Ibid.   18. Ibid.
19. Toledo _Blade_, ibid.
20. Effrat, Louis. "New York Eleven Is Victor, 21 to 9." New York _Times_. October 15, 1956.
21. Effrat, Louis. "New York Victor at Stadium, 20-3" New York _Times_. October 29, 1956.
22. Ibid.   23. Ibid.   24. Ibid.
25. Effrat, Louis. "New York Gains 6th Victory, 23-10." New York _Times_. November 11, 1956.
26. Tuckner, Ibid. 27. Ibid.
28. Daley, Arthur. "Flatter Than a Bear-Rug," Sports of The Times. New York _Times_. December 31, 1956.
29. Effrat, Louis. "Fans See Chicago Bow, 47-7." New York _Times_. December 31, 1956.
30. Ibid.   32. Ibid.
33. Gotteher, Barry. The Football Giants of New York: The History of Professional Football's Most Fabulous Dynasty. Putnam Publishing, 1963. p. 239, 240.

Chapter II. Building a Career

1. Gotteher, Barry. The Football Giants at New York - The History of Professional Football's Most Fabulous Dynasty. Putnam Publishing, 1963. p. 256.
2. Ibid., p. 257.
3. Smith, Don. The New York Football Giants, Inc. p. 2.
4. "Giants Still Hope Dec. 14 Date With Browns Will Decide Title," Pro News. November 18, 1958. p. 3.
5. Effrat, Louis. "Defense Excels in 2d-10 Triumph," New York _Times_. December 1, 1958.
6. Whittingham, Richard. The Giants - From The Polo Grounds to Super Bowl XXI - An Illustrated History. Harper and Rowe, 1987. p. 104.
7. Ibid.   8. Ibid.   9. Ibid.
10. Great Teams' Great Years: New York Giants. December 28, 1958. p. 64.
11. Effrat, Louis. "Colts Beat Giants, Win in Overtime," New York _Times_. December 29, 1958. [Front page].

Chapter III. Television Saw It

1.   Whittingham, Richard. <u>New York Football Giants. From the Polo Grounds to Superbowl XXI: An Illustrated History.</u> Harper and Rowe, 1987. p. 112.

2.   White, Gordon S., Jr. "Giant Man-In-Motion Blocker Throws Eagle Line Off Balance," New York <u>Times</u>. October 19, 1959.

3.   <u>Ibid</u>.

4.   Tuckner, Howard M. "Svare's Blitz of Ball Carrier Puts New York on Victory Path," New York <u>Times</u>. November 2, 1959.

5.   Smith, Don. <u>The New York Football Giants, Inc</u>. 1960. p. 2.

5a.   Effrat, Louis. "Conerley's Passes Lead to 48-7 Rout!" New York <u>Times</u>. December 7, 1959.

6.   <u>Ibid</u>.

7.   White, Gordon. "Giants Failure To Get First Down Was Key To Game, According to Ewbank," New York <u>Times</u>. December 27, 1959.

8.   <u>Ibid</u>.   9.   <u>Ibid</u>.

10.   White, Gordon S. Jr. October 19, 1959. <u>Ibid</u>.

Chapter IV: Trades and Fades

1.   Teague, Robert L. "New York Takes Opener, 21-19," New York <u>Times</u>. September 25, 1960.

2.   Effrat, Louis. "Giants Upset Browns in Snow: Line Play Marks 17 to 13 Victory." New York <u>Times</u>. November 7, 1960.

3.   Sheenan, Joseph M. "31-31 Draw Drops New York to 3D," New York <u>Times</u>. December 5, 1960.

4.   Klobuchar, Jim. "It's Triplett's Turn Sunday For Shot At Viking Fullback!" Minneapolis <u>Morning Tribune</u>. August 31, 1962.

5.   <u>Ibid</u>.   6.   <u>Ibid</u>.

7.   Heaton, Charles. "Triplett Hopes To Pair With Brown," The Cleveland <u>Plain Dealer</u>. July 13, 1963.

8.   <u>Ibid</u>.

Chapter V. Little Brother Grows Up

1.   Kerch, Bill. "Big Red Obtains Giants Triplett." St. Louis <u>Globe Dispatch</u>. May 11, 1962.

2.   Posen, Bob. "Big Red Gets Giants Bill Triplett, Future Draft Choice for Guglielmi," St. Louis <u>Post-Dispatch</u>. May 10, 1962. p. 1E.

3.   <u>Ibid</u>.

4.   Morrison, Robert. "Still One Over NFL's Limit of 38 Players." St. Louis <u>Post-Dispatch</u>. September 4, 1962. p. 6B.

5.   Morrison, Robert. [No title] <u>Ibid</u>. October 29, 1962.

6.   Morrison, Robert. "49er's Roll-Outs Full Cards; Interceptions, Fumble Also Hurt," St. Louise <u>Post-Dispatch</u>. November 26, 1962. p. 4B.

7.   <u>Ibid</u>.

8.   Morrison, Robert. "Johnson's Throwing Big Lift," St. Louis <u>Post-Dispatch</u>. December 19, 1962.

9.   <u>Ibid</u>.

10.   St. Louis <u>Post-Dispatch</u>. "Ruling Against AFL Upheld by Court." September 23, 1963. p. 4C.

11.   Considine, Tim. <u>The Language of Sport</u>. World Almanac Publica-

tions: New York, 1983. p. 125.
12. Morrison, Robert. "Pittsburgh Emerges Unbeaten," St. Louis <u>Post-Dispatch</u>. September 30, 1963. p.1.
13. Ibid.
14. "Detroit Trades Colavito to KC," St. Louis <u>Post-Dispatch</u>. November 18, 1963.
15. "Rozelle Defends Decision To Play." <u>Ibid</u>., November 25, 1963.

Chapter VI. Erase That Year

1. Clemente, Dick. "Giants' Dream About Triplett Repeats Itself." <u>Newsday</u>. July 27, 1967.
2. Olperman, Tyrav. "Between You'n Me," Newspaper Interprise Association. 1966.
3. Kerch, Bill. "Bill Triplett Longs to Play," St. Louis <u>Globe-Democrat</u>. September 9, 1964.
4. Ibid.   5. Ibid.   6. Ibid.
7. Ibid.   8. Ibid.
9. Broeg, Bob. "Bill Triplett's Red-Letter Day." St. Louis <u>Post-Dispatch</u>. August 27, 1965.
10. Ibid.
11. Morrison, Robert. "Comeback Triplett Has Triple Objective." <u>Ibid</u>. July 1965.
12. Ibid.
13. Morrison, Robert. "Big Red Find Victory Rout," St. Louis <u>Post-Dispatch</u>. September 27, 1965.
14. Ibid.   15. Ibid.   16. Ibid.
17. Morrison, Robert. "Cards Did Everything--Giants Scared," St. Louis <u>Post-Dispatch</u>. November 1, 1965.
18. "Browns Take Title With Payoff Punch!" <u>Post-Dispatch</u> Wire Service. November 29, 1965.
19. "Bill Triplett: Comeback Cardinal." <u>Ibid</u>., 1966.
20. Ibid.

Chapter VII: Rehabilitation

1. Rice, Jack. [No title: St. Louis Police Department]. St. Louis <u>Post Dispatch</u>. February 27, 1966.
2. Ibid.   3. Ibid.
4. "Triplett Scored Big Making Friends," <u>Police Journal</u>. August, 1966.
5. Ibid.
6. Rice, Jack. Ibid.
7. Olperman, Tyrav. "Between You'n Me," Newspaper Interprise Association. 1966.
8. Ibid.
9. Flynn, George L. and Red Smith. <u>Vince Lombardi on Football</u>. George L. Flynn, ed. Introduction, Red Smith. Galahad Books: New York, 1973. p. 16.
10. Saylor, Jack. "Triplett Named Captain of Lions' Specialty Squads," Detroit <u>Free Press</u>. October 22, 1971.
11. Ibid.   12. Ibid.

Chapter VIII. De-Fense!

1. Forbes, Dick. "Miami U's Bob Babich Misses His Old School," <u>Enquirer</u>, July 1969.
2. "Babich Ready for Grid Comeback," Cleveland <u>Plain Dealer</u>, Special Edition. 1970.
3. <u>Ibid</u>.   4. <u>Ibid</u>.
5. Ossino, Del. "The Pros Like Miami's Babich." The Cincinnati <u>Enquirer</u>. 1969. p. 50.
6. Young, Dick. "Young Ideas," New York <u>Daily News</u>. August 28, 1969.
7. <u>Ibid</u>.   8. <u>Ibid</u>.   9. <u>Ibid</u>.
10. <u>Plain Dealer</u> Special Edition. <u>Ibid</u>.
11. <u>Ibid</u>.   12. <u>Ibid</u>.
13. Flynn, George L. and Red Smith. <u>Vince Lombardi on Football</u>. George L. Flynn, ed. Introduction, Red Smith. Galahad Books: New York, 1973. Vol. II, p. 46.

Chapter IX. Outside Shift

1. "News From the San Diego Chargers," publicity release. Wynn. Jerry and Walter Hoye, Dir. Public Relations. November 23, 1971.
2. <u>Ibid</u>.
3. "Garrett Helps Chargers Stun Vikings, 30-14," Los Angeles <u>Times</u>. November, 1971.
4. Knapick, John. Personal interview with Ron Rotunno, February 7, 1991.
5. Gill, Sloko. Personal interview with Ron Rotunno, February 7, 1991.
6. Flynn, George L. and Red Smith. <u>Vince Lombardi on Football</u>. George L. Flynn, ed. Introduction, Red Smith Galahad Books: New York, 1973. Vol. II, p. 43.
7. Maule, Tex. "The Dirty Dozen Clean Up," <u>Pro Football</u>. September, 1972. p. 72.
8. Oates, Bob. "Gabriel, Defense Account For Four-TD Burst," Los Angeles <u>Times</u>. September 18, 1972.
9. San Diego, AP Release. "Chargers, Hit by 94-Yard Opening Kickoff Return, Bounce Back, 37-14." 1972.
10. "Chargers Tie Raiders as Blanda's Kick Fails," Los Angeles <u>Times</u>. September, 1972.
11. Bisheff, Steve. "Is Strong Side For Babich," Los Angeles <u>Times</u>. November, 1972.
12. <u>Ibid</u>.   13. <u>Ibid</u>.   13a. <u>Ibid</u>.
14. <u>Ibid</u>.   15. <u>Ibid</u>.
16. "Pittsburgh Wins Title After Waiting 40 Years," Los Angeles <u>Times</u>. December, 1972.
17. <u>Ibid</u>.   18. <u>Ibid</u>.
19. Flynn and Smith. <u>Ibid</u>.

Chapter X: Back to Ohio

1. Heaton, Chuck. "Browns Get Babich For Draft Choices, Line backer says 'Hope I'm Worth It.'" Cleveland <u>Plain Dealer</u>. September 6, 1973.

2. "Browns and Babich Happy Over Trade," Cleveland Plain Dealer.
    September 6, 1973.
3. Ibid.   4. Ibid.
5. "Babich Wants To Be No. 1," ___________. September 17, 1973.
6. Ibid.   7. Ibid.   8. Ibid.   9. Ibid.
9a. "Skorich Warns Browns, Praise." Cleveland Plain Dealer.
    September 12, 1973.
10. Ibid.
11. "Babich Wants To Be," Ibid.
12. Ibid.   13. Ibid.   14. Ibid.
15. "Skorich: Theft Turned Tide." Cleveland Plain Dealer.
    October 1, 1973.
16. Ibid.
17. Coughlin, Dan. "Played As Well As They Could," Cleveland Plain
    Dealer. October, 1973.
18. ___________. "Thriller Awaits Phipps On Film." Cleveland Plain
    Dealer. November 28, 1973.
19. Ibid.
20. "More Cheers For Babich," Cleveland Plain Dealer.
    November, 1973.
21. Ibid.   22. Ibid.   23. Ibid.
24. Ibid.   25. Ibid.
26. Heaton, Chuck. "Browns Sign Babich To 3-Year Contract,"
    Cleveland Plain Dealer. June 14, 1974.
27. Ibid.   28. Ibid.   29. Ibid.
30. Ibid.   31. Ibid.   32. Heaton, Chuck. "Victory,
    Defense Cheers," Cleveland Plain Dealer. September 23, 1974.
    p. 1F, 2F.
31. Ibid.   32. Ibid.   33. Ibid.
34. ___________. "Cardinals Clout Browns," Cleveland Plain Dealer.
    September 30, 1974.
35. Ibid.
36. ___________. "Defense Crumbles," Cleveland Plain Dealer.
    October 14, 1974.
37. Ibid.   38. Ibid.
39. ___________. "Browns Gave Us Big Scare, Says Steelers' Head
    Coach." Cleveland Plain Dealer. October 21, 1974.
40. ___________. "Sipe Rallies Browns, Enlivens Post-Game
    Banter." Cleveland Plain Dealer. December, 1974.

CHAPTER XI: WHILE YOU'RE AHEAD

1. Public Relations Department, Cleveland Browns. News Release;
    Summer, 1976 [covering previous year].
2. Ibid.   3. Ibid.
4. Press Release. "Sober? Babich Expects Winning Season."
    Cleveland Plain Dealer. November 15, 1975.
5. Coughlin, Dan. "Browns' GM Threatens Players." Cleveland
    Plain Dealer. September 1975.
6. Ibid.   7. Ibid.
8. Coughlin, Dan. "Browns Linebackers Cut Down Chargers."
    Cleveland Plain Dealer. October 25, 1976.

9. __________. "Babich Succeeds in Besting Bergey." Cleveland <u>Plain Dealer</u>. November 15, 1976.
10. <u>Ibid</u>.
11. Heaton, Chuck. "Special Teams, Defense Praised." Cleveland <u>Plain Dealer</u>. October 1976.
12. Webster, Chuck. "Good Defense Key to Browns' Win." Cleveland <u>Plain Dealer</u>. November 1976.
13. <u>Ibid</u>.   14. <u>Ibid</u>.
15. Public Relations Department, Cleveland Browns News Release; Summer 1977 [covering previous year].
16. <u>Ibid</u>.

EPILOGUE: TODAY

1. Flynn, George L. and Red Smith. <u>Vince Lombardi on Football</u>. Galahad Books: New York, 1973.

STEEL VALLEY BOOKS

Ohio • Pennsylvania